WOODROW WILSON
AND THE WORLD OF TODAY

It is by the widening of vision that nations, as men, grow and are made great. We need not fear the expanding scene. It was plain destiny that we should come to this, and if we have kept our ideals clear, unmarred, commanding through the great century and the moving scenes that made us a nation, we may keep them also through the century that shall see us a great power in the world. Let us put our leading characters at the front; let us pray that vision may come with power; let us ponder our duties like men of conscience and temper our ambitions like men who seek to serve, not to subdue, the world; let us lift our thoughts to the level of the great tasks that await us, and bring a great age in with the coming of our day of strength.

WOODROW WILSON, "The Ideals of America,"
Atlantic Monthly, XC (December, 1902),
721-734.

Woodrow Wilson
and The World of Today

Essays by
Arthur S. Link
William L. Langer
Eric F. Goldman

Edited by
Arthur P. Dudden

Philadelphia
UNIVERSITY OF PENNSYLVANIA PRESS

Manufactured in the United States of America by
Book Craftsmen Associates, Inc., New York

Foreword

On the one hundred and twenty-fifth anniversary of the battle of Trenton, December 26, 1901, Woodrow Wilson, then Professor of Jurisprudence at Princeton University, assured his listeners, who were gathered to celebrate Washington's surprise victory over the Hessians, that the spirit of those revolutionary days was not dead, but lived on into the twentieth century. As Wilson spoke, something of the prophet came forward in him to mingle with the historian and the political scientist, and to supply, if only for a fleeting moment, a vision of the time not far distant when the speaker himself would shoulder the burdens of the United States, in turn to leave an indelible mark upon the world. With flights of stirring oratory, Wilson blended the American past with the present in a moving panorama. The nation had not forgotten the spirit of the old days, he said. "Its past it feels to have been but the prelude and earnest of its present. It is from its memories of days old and new that it gets its sense of identity, takes its spirit of action, assures itself of its power and its capacity, and knows its place in the world." But Wilson seemed concerned more with the present and the future than with the past. He reminded his audience that mighty transformations had endlessly reshaped their beloved country since 1776. "The battle of Trenton was not more signifi-

cant than the battle of Manila," he went on. "The nation that was one hundred and twenty-five years in the
making has now stepped forth into the open arena of
the world."

"I ask you to stand with me at this new turning-point
of our life," Wilson urged, "that we may look before
and after, and judge ourselves alike in the light of that
old battle fought here in these streets, and in the light of
all the mighty processes of our history that have followed. We cannot too often give ourselves such challenge of self-examination. It will hearten, it will steady,
it will moralize us to reassess our hopes, restate our
ideals, and make manifest to ourselves again the principles and the purposes upon which we act. We are else
without chart upon a novel voyage."

In retrospect, Woodrow Wilson's locating of himself
and the American nation at a crucial crossroads of civilization revealed something of that remarkable talent of
his for perceiving and directing the juxtapositions of
men and events. Even in 1901, he seemed to be steering
himself and his generation toward "a rendezvous with
destiny," long before Franklin Delano Roosevelt cap-
tured this phrase.

Within less than ten years, he became Governor of
New Jersey, and put the academic world firmly behind
him. Then, in 1913, he and his magnetic New Freedom
program of reform entered the White House after an
exciting three-cornered race for the presidency, a contest which was fought almost exclusively to determine
the most satisfactory ways of asserting popular, democratic control over America's sprawling new industrial
society. At the end of his first administration, Wilson
was able to look back upon an impressive list of progressive accomplishments: tariff reduction, the Federal

Reserve System of banking, the Federal Trade Commission, new antitrust legislation, a network of Federal Farm Loan banks, improved working standards for merchant seamen, legislation outlawing child labor in interstate commerce (later invalidated as unconstitutional by the Supreme Court), an eight-hour day for railway employees, and more of a similar nature. Meanwhile the domestic process became hopelessly engulfed by the issues of the first World War. So much so, in fact, that the election issues of 1916 did not primarily devolve upon reform, but became absorbed by problems of military preparedness from one corner or pacifistic clamor from another.

Again Woodrow Wilson rode the crest of the wave of history in the making. Before his second inauguration Germany had commenced her calculated campaign of unrestricted undersea warfare, which by mid-April, 1917, brought the United States into the fray on the side of Great Britain and France. These developments were ironic as well as kaleidoscopic, in view of Wilson's recent re-election appeal based in considerable part on the popular slogan: "He kept us out of war!" All of which was quickly forgotten, however, in the excitement of the new adventure. Led by President Wilson, the American people, as though in fulfillment of his own remarks spoken years before at Trenton, "now stepped forth into the open arena of the world." And there they remained, while a mighty war machine was created out of the untapped potentials of the nation and until victory became theirs amidst delirious happiness in the armistice of 1918. Optimistically now the world sat down to construct the peace settlements, ostensibly to be based firmly upon the principles of Wilson's Fourteen Points. Indeed this was the finest hour of all. But the tragic unfolding of the Peace of Versailles revealed how deep were the ravages of war. Nowhere to be seen was there a world made safe for democracy and human progress. Instead the future lay dark and foreboding. European civilization was economically unsettled, socially embittered, politically wounded, ripe for totalitarianism and more war. This time Woodrow Wilson knew bitter defeat. He was cast aside politically, while at the same time he was wrecked physically by exertions which overtaxed his strength. But the cruelest blow of all was the repudiation of his beloved League of Nations by his own people, those whom he had led to the pinnacles of world power and prestige. Nothing remained for him but his own death.

The years passed. The League of Nations failed before the onslaught of the dictators and because of the feebleness of its friends. A second great World War began out of the ashes and discords of the first, as Woodrow Wilson had foretold it would if the peace settlements were not made thoroughly secure. Once again, the United States played a central part. This time the nation's leaders earnestly sought to avoid what they conceived to have been the earlier mistakes which had led to the overthrow of Woodrow Wilson's principles. So assiduously did they attempt to right earlier wrongs that it seemed at times as if Wilson's spirit was standing nearby to set matters right at long last. For it was clear indeed, as World War II neared its end and the United Nations prepared to undertake even greater tasks than the League of Nations had laid down, that among his own countrymen Woodrow Wilson's influence was stronger than it had been at any time since his death. This was evident in the determination of the United States to participate in the United Nations from its in-

ception. It has stayed evident in the determination of
the majority of Americans to stick to their U.N. membership through all the difficult periods since 1945.
Meanwhile, on the domestic front through years of depression and recovery, of war and social turmoil, it was
clear also that Woodrow Wilson's example of powerful
exercise of the executive office of President was now the
accepted pattern of national leadership. Whenever
strong leadership was lacking, the nation appeared to
drift alarmingly. Whenever it was present, there was
direction and accomplishment. As Wilson had said at
Trenton: "We are else without chart upon a novel
voyage." But Woodrow Wilson's vision of the future had
provided mankind with a chart to explore the world of
today.

Inasmuch as Wilson's teaching career began at Bryn
Mawr College, it seemed appropriate that this college
should play an early part in the nationwide celebrations
of the centennial of his birth. A conference was held on
the campus January 5 and 6, 1956, with the over-all
theme, "Woodrow Wilson and the World of Today."
Its purpose was a reappraisal of what the career, ideas,
and principles of Woodrow Wilson signified for mankind everywhere. As Wilson himself said: "We cannot
too often give ourselves such challenge of self-examination." This volume of four essays is a contribution to
that end.

In addition to the three distinguished scholars whose
lectures appear herein, many persons and institutions
joined to make the conference a memorable occasion.
To all these, Bryn Mawr College expresses its sincere
appreciation. Special gratitude must be expressed to the
Woodrow Wilson Foundation for its counsel and financial assistance. To my colleagues of the faculty centen-

nial committee, Roger H. Wells and Gertrude Leighton, I am grateful for their wholehearted co-operation and invaluable contributions.

ARTHUR P. DUDDEN, *Chairman*
Woodrow Wilson Centennial Committee
Bryn Mawr College

December 28, 1956

Contents

WOODROW WILSON

AND THE WORLD OF TODAY

Woodrow Wilson: The Philosophy, Methods, and Impact of Leadership*

ARTHUR S. LINK

Professor of History, Northwestern University

Few men have come to the presidency with bolder schemes of leadership or made greater contributions to the development of effective national government in the United States than Woodrow Wilson. Unusual circumstances enabled him for a time to demonstrate conclusively that the President has it within his power, not only to be the chief spokesman of the American people, but also to destroy the wall between the executive and legislative branches in the formulation and adoption of legislative programs. He accomplished this feat, not accidentally, but because he willed to be a strong leader and used his opportunities wisely for a time; and historians a century hence might well rate his expansion and perfection of the powers of the presidency as his most lasting contribution.

---

* Parts of this essay have appeared in Arthur S. Link, *Wilson: The New Freedom,* published by the Princeton University Press, 1956, and are reprinted by permission of the Press.

It is altogether appropriate that we should take note of Wilson's achievements and permanent contributions to American political practice at this time, for the nation and the world need the kind of leadership that he gave, even more today than they needed it in Wilson's own day. Woodrow Wilson was born nearly one hundred years ago in Staunton, Virginia, and during the following months institutions and organizations all over the United States will celebrate the centennial of his birth by trying to recall his life and ideals. It is also fitting that Bryn Mawr College should play a significant part in this nation-wide assessment, for it was here, in 1885, that Wilson began his long and distinguished academic career.

The key to a knowledge of Wilson's contributions lies, first of all, in an understanding of his philosophy of leadership. Since his undergraduate days at Princeton he had been intrigued by a study of politics, which he interpreted largely in terms of the behavior of great men. Immersed in studying the development of Anglo-American democracy and imbued by Christian beliefs, he had, early in his career, concluded that the ideal leader was the man strong in moral fiber, determined in purpose, and audacious in vision, who could lead his people forward along the road of progressive development.

"In what, then, does political leadership consist?" he asked in what was perhaps his most self-revealing address. "It is leadership in conduct, and leadership in conduct must discern and strengthen the tendencies that make for development. . . . I do not believe that any man can lead who does not act, whether it be consciously or unconsciously, under the impulse of a profound sympathy with those whom he leads. . . . Such men incarnate the consciences of the men whom they rule . . .

[and are] quick to know and to do the things that the hour and his nation need."[1]

Such was the ideal leader, but how could he function best in the arena of national politics in a democracy like the United States? This was the question to which Wilson addressed his main attention between the late 1870's and the early 1900's, and the answer that he gave was conditioned by his admiration of British political leaders, particularly of William E. Gladstone, and the parliamentary system, and by the extraordinary dearth of leadership in American national politics between Lincoln and Theodore Roosevelt.

The 1880's and 1890's in the United States were a time of almost absolute congressional supremacy and of Presidents who were the captives of Congressional and party machines, not leaders of public opinion and makers of Federal policies. It was perhaps inevitable, therefore, that the young Wilson, while an undergraduate at Princeton, should have dreamed of a political career in the Senate, not in the White House; and that the young scholar in his early writings and addresses, particularly in his most famous book, *Congressional Government: A Study in American Politics* (1885), should have written off the President as a useless fifth wheel in the American constitutional system and called for the adoption of the British Cabinet system, which concentrated leadership and responsibility in an executive body responsible to the legislature.

Actually, Wilson never completely abandoned the belief that the parliamentary system provided the best vehicle for responsible leadership in a democracy. As late as 1913 we find him writing that sooner or later the

[1] Woodrow Wilson, *Leaders of Men* (Princeton, 1952), pp. 43, 53–54, 60.

President "must be made answerable to opinion in a somewhat more informal and intimate fashion—answerable, it may be, to the Houses whom he seeks to lead, either personally or through a Cabinet, as well as to the people for whom they speak."[2] Moreover, Wilson's plan to resign in order to allow his Republican opponent, Charles Evans Hughes, to assume the presidency immediately after the election of 1916, should Hughes win the election; Wilson's ill-fated appeal for the election of a Democratic Congress in 1918; and his tragic attempt to make the election of 1920 a "solemn referendum" on the League issue were all later examples of Wilson's efforts to adapt the parliamentary system to American practice.

And yet we can overemphasize this point. It is more important to remember that Wilson's views on the possibility of effective leadership in the presidential-Congressional system changed fundamentally during the early 1900's in response to two of the most important political developments of the time. One of these was the emergence of the United States to world power around the turn of the century, a development that Wilson knew would have a profound impact upon the location of authority and the system of leadership in the Federal government. "Much the most important change to be noticed," he wrote in the preface to the fifteenth edition of *Congressional Government* in 1900, "is the result of the war with Spain upon the lodgement and exercise of power within our federal system: the greatly increased power and opportunity for constructive statesmanship

[2] Wilson to A. Mitchell Palmer, February 5, 1913, in Ray Stannard Baker and William E. Dodd (eds.), *The Public Papers of Woodrow Wilson, The New Democracy* (2 vols., New York, 1926), I, 24.

given the President, by the plunge into international politics and into the administration of distant dependencies, which has been that war's most striking and momentous consequence."[3]

A second development that compelled Wilson to view the potentialities of presidential leadership in a more favorable light was the revivification of the presidency by Theodore Roosevelt, who demonstrated the potential powers of the Chief Executive by asserting a national leadership through control of public opinion. Indeed, as a direct consequence of Roosevelt's success in marshaling public opinion and bludgeoning Congress into adopting significant reform legislation, Wilson had come to view the presidency in a new light by the time he delivered his last scholarly lectures—a series presented at Columbia University in 1907 and published under the title of *Constitutional Government in the United States* in 1908. Wilson now saw the President as potentially a powerful party leader and national spokesman who, by appealing to the people over the heads of Congress, as Roosevelt had done, might exercise a strong influence over the course of legislation. The President, Wilson asserted, "is . . . the political leader of the nation, or has it in his choice to be. The nation as a whole has chosen him, and is conscious that it has no other political spokesman. His is the only national voice in affairs. Let him once win the admiration and confidence of the country, and no other single force can withstand him, no combination of forces will easily overpower him. . . . If he rightly interpret the national thought and boldly insist upon it, he is irresistible."[4]

[3] *Congressional Government: A Study in American Politics* (15th ed.; Boston and New York, 1900 [?]), p. xi.

[4] Woodrow Wilson, *Constitutional Government in the United States* (New York, 1908), p. 68.

Events between 1907 and 1913, notably Roosevelt's continued success and Taft's failure as popular leaders, only reinforced Wilson's new view of the President. The President, he wrote early in 1913, "is expected by the Nation to be the leader of his party as well as the Chief Executive officer of the Government, and the country will take no excuses from him. He must play the part and play it successfully or lose the country's confidence. He must be prime minister, as much concerned with the guidance of legislation as with the just and orderly execution of law, and he is the spokesman of the Nation in everything, even in the most momentous and most delicate dealings of the Government with foreign nations."[5]

Even before he was inaugurated in 1913, moreover, Wilson as President-elect let it be clearly understood that he would put his new views into practice. "He is not without party sympathies and not insensible to party obligations," one reporter wrote after an interview with Wilson in January 1913, "but he is the president; and in the end it is his judgment that will prevail, as he intends to make it, in the settlement of all matters that come before him for consideration. . . . He has readily assumed all responsibility that has been given him. He feels himself capable. He has faith in himself. And he looks upon himself as an instrument for bringing about certain reforms and for ameliorating certain conditions. The predestined idea is not remote from his thought and conclusion."[6]

Woodrow Wilson entered the White House not only

[5] Wilson to A. M. Palmer, February 5, 1913, in R. S. Baker and W. E. Dodd (eds.), *The New Democracy*, I, 23–24.

[6] Samuel G. Blythe, "Our New President," *Saturday Evening Post*, CLXXXV (March 1, 1913), 4.

equipped in theory but also experienced in leadership as president of Princeton University and Governor of New Jersey. In fact, during a decade of apprenticeship from 1902 to 1912 he had worked out and applied all the methods of leadership that he would use so successfully after 1912. Using the techniques of a prime minister, he had led the trustees and faculty of Princeton University in effecting such far-reaching changes in curriculum and teaching methods that almost overnight Princeton had been transformed from a backward provincial college into a leader among institutions of higher learning in the United States. Exploiting the full powers of the governorship, he had seized control of his party after his election in 1910 and transformed his state from a stronghold of corporate privilege into a leader in progressive reform. And his success had catapulted him into the leadership of the Democratic party in the nation and soon into the White House.

Wilson's success as a leader of domestic reform in state and nation from 1910 to 1917 stemmed in part from his methods, which we will soon describe, and in part from the extraordinary political circumstances prevailing during these years, which have often been overlooked in making an assessment. To begin with, the reform impulses and movements that had shattered party alignments in the 1890's and disrupted the Republican party during Taft's administration were pulsating at an even faster tempo during the years of Wilson's governorship and his first presidential term. The majority public opinion, Republican as well as Democratic, demanded tariff, tax, and currency reform, a program aimed at establishing public control of railroads, utilities, banks, and manufacturing industries, and increased public assistance to and protection for farmers, workers, and underprivileged groups. Thus Wilson's chief task, which he performed superbly, was the relatively easy one of synthesizing the majority political thought of his time and of giving leadership to an already aroused public opinion.

Wilson's task as President was lightened, moreover, by the peculiar situation that prevailed in Congress during his first term. To begin with, there was the absence of any rival powerful leader in the legislative branch. In 1910 a group of young rebels, led by Representative George W. Norris of Nebraska, had sheared the Speaker of the House, Joseph G. Cannon of Illinois, of his almost absolute control over legislation by adopting new rules depriving the Speaker of the right to route bills and to appoint committees. The effect of this revolution was to destroy one of the most effective counterpoises to presidential power and to create a vacuum in leadership which Wilson speedily filled.

In addition, because of the disruption of the Republican party from 1910 to 1916 the Democrats enjoyed large majorities in the House of Representatives and workable majorities in the Senate strengthened by insurgent Republican support. But an even more important factor in facilitating Wilson's leadership was the character of the Democratic membership of Congress during this period. To begin with, one hundred and fourteen of the two hundred and ninety Democratic members of the House in 1913 had been elected for the first time the year before. Eager to please, because their future careers depended in large measure upon patronage and the administration's success, they were like putty in the President's hands. Secondly, the veteran Southerners in both houses knew that the fate of their party depended upon their success in satisfying the national demand for reform; they, too, willingly accepted Wilson's leadership. Thirdly, probably a majority of the senators, Democratic and Republican, were advanced progressives, many of whom were at first in closer touch with reform sentiment than Wilson himself. In these favorable circumstances, it was comparatively simple for Wilson to be the most effective of all leaders in the American constitutional system—the spokesman and mediator of a co-operative Congressional majority.

Wilson's least obvious but in a sense most important advantage was the fact that he was a newcomer in national politics and the leader of the Democratic party during a time when it was consciously attempting to transform itself from a sectional, largely agrarian party into a national organization representative of all sections and classes. Unlike Bryan, Wilson was relatively free from personal obligations accumulated over long years of political activity. Unlike Roosevelt, he was not bound by party commitments and policies that had become tantamount to ingrained traditions.

It is no derogation of Wilson's contribution to describe these circumstances that facilitated his strong leadership on the national scene from 1913 to 1917, for his contribution in techniques was substantial enough. His first technique of leadership was to assert the position of spokesman of the American people and to use public opinion as a spur on Congress. Theodore Roosevelt had demonstrated the usefulness of this method, but Wilson used it to greater advantage and made it inevitable that any future President would be powerful only in so far as he established intimate communication with the people and spoke effectively for them.

His chief instruments in winning a position as national spokesman were of course oratory and public mes-

ges, by means of which he gave voice to the highest
aspirations, first of the American people, and then, during the war and afterward, of the people of the world.
He was a virtuoso and a spellbinder during a time when
the American people admired oratory above all other
political skills. But as a spellbinder he appealed chiefly
to men's minds and spirits, and only infrequently to
their passions; and it is doubtful if any leader in American history since Lincoln has succeeded so well in com-
municating the ideals that the American people have in
their better moments tried to live by.

This was true because Wilson was a romantic moral-
ist, who, using the poet's hyperbole to express political
and moral truth, raised every issue and conflict to a high
stage upon which the human drama was being played
out. Were the citizens of Trenton about to vote upon
the adoption of commission government? Then they
were being given an opportunity to show the world
whether Americans were capable of enlightened self-
government! Were the American people about to enter
a world war? Then they were privileged to give their
blood and treasure to make the world safe for democracy and to extend the dominion of righteousness
throughout the earth!

There were times when the spellbinder was so ex-
hilarated that he said things he did not mean or his
verbiage obscured the ideas that he sought to express.
There were also times, during flights of fancy mainly in
extemporaneous speeches, when his oratory was like a
symphony, meant to be heard and felt emotionally but
not understood. There were even dangers in an excess
of nobility and moral vision, because there was always
the temptation to idealize unpleasant situations and
necessities, and this in turn sometimes led Wilson to

romanticize objectives and to refuse to confront hard realities. A discerning contemporary analyzed the faults and dangers of Wilson's oratory, as follows:

"Mr. Wilson seems to be one of those people who shuffle off their mortal coil as soon as they take pen in hand. They become tremendously noble. They write as the monuments of great men might write. They write only upon brass, and for nothing shorter than a millennium. They utter nothing which might sound trivial at the Last Judgment, or embarrass them in the most august company. . . .

"It is the quality of Mr. Wilson's thinking to make even the most concrete things seem like abstractions. Technically he is perfectly aware that ideals are good for what they are good for, in the real world of moving men; actually he conveys only the most remote view of that world. His mind is like a light which destroys the outlines of what it plays upon; there is much illumination, but you see very little."[7]

The criticism was not capricious, and yet the conviction remains that Wilson as an orator was nearly incomparable at his best, that he was a sensitive poet who not only intuitively absorbed national political ideals but was also able to translate them into words so lofty and inspiring that they perhaps helped to change the course of history. Certainly the man who could say "This is not a day of triumph; it is a day of dedication. Here muster, not the forces of party, but the forces of humanity. Men's hearts wait upon us; men's lives hang in the balance; men's hopes call upon us to say what we will do," or "The right is more precious than peace, and we shall fight for the things which we have always

[7] Herbert Croly, "The Other-Worldliness of Wilson," *New Republic,* II (March 27, 1915), 194–195.

carried nearest our hearts,—for democracy, for the right of those who submit to authority to have a voice in their own Governments, for the rights and liberties of small nations, for a universal dominion of right by such a concert of free peoples as shall bring peace and safety to all nations and make the world itself at last free"— surely the man who could say these things could speak with the tongue of an angel to recall the visions lost in the struggle for wealth and power.

In addition to his use of oratory and formal public speeches, Wilson maintained an intimate relationship with the people by frequent informal statements and appeals in the press. He first used the technique as Governor of New Jersey, during his fierce struggles with the Democratic bosses of that state; he employed the method with equal success during his first term as President. During the controversy over tariff reform in 1913, for example, he destroyed a powerful lobby by simply denouncing and exposing it. He neutralized the opposition of certain financial leaders to his plan for banking and currency reform by forthright appeals to the people. For a time he even tried to conduct diplomacy through the newspapers.

On the other hand, we should add a word of reservation here about the manner in which Wilson used this method of public leadership. So firmly did the President control Congress during his first term that only upon one important occasion—during the debate over military and naval expansion in 1916—did he appeal to the people over the head of Congress, as Theodore Roosevelt had so often done. During the period 1913 to 1917 Wilson's public appeals were almost always directed at building popular support for his party and program against the assaults of private interests and the Republican opposition.

Wilson made his most significant contribution to the growth of the power of the presidential office, not through exploitation of national leadership, for in this regard he merely perfected a method already highly developed by Roosevelt, but rather in the way in which he took control of his party in Congress and succeeded in fusing the powers of the executive and legislative branches in his own person.

He began soon after his inauguration. On March 9, 1913, White House spokesmen announced that the new President would help frame important legislation; ten days later these same spokesmen added that Wilson would confer frequently with Democratic leaders in the President's Room in the Capitol. But Wilson's most spectacular assertion of leadership came soon afterward, when he delivered his message on tariff reform in person before the two houses on April 8, 1913.

It is difficult for a generation accustomed to seeing the President appear frequently before the Congress to understand the symbolic significance of Wilson's act. Thomas Jefferson had abandoned the custom of appearing before Congress on the ground that it resembled too much the King's speech from the throne; and Jefferson's precedent had become an unwritten part of the Constitution during the following century. The White House's announcement on April 6, 1913, that Wilson would deliver his tariff message in person, therefore, evoked great indignation among the legislators, especially among Democrats who revered the Jeffersonian symbols. "I for one very much regret the President's course," exclaimed Senator John Sharp Williams of Mississippi on April 7. ". . . I am sorry to see revived the old Federalistic custom of speeches from the throne. . . . I regret all this cheap and tawdry imitation of English royalty."[8]

Going before Congress, however, was Wilson's way of telling the country that he meant to destroy the wall that had so long divided the executive from the legislative arm. "I think that this is the only dignified way for the President to address Congress at the opening of a session, instead of sending the address to be read perfunctorily in the clerk's familiar tone of voice," he explained in a public reply to his critics. "I thought that the dignified and natural thing was to read it."[9] And when he appeared before the joint session the following day, he added:

"I am very glad indeed to have this opportunity to address the two Houses directly and to verify for myself the impression that the President of the United States is a person, not a mere department of the Government hailing Congress from some isolated island of jealous power, sending messages, not speaking naturally and with his own voice—that he is a human being trying to co-operate with other human beings in a common service."[10]

Less obvious and well known were the methods that Wilson used to establish control over the Democratic membership of Congress. Even before he was inaugurated, he had to choose between leadership of a Democratic-insurgent Republican coalition of progressives or

[8] *New York Times,* April 8, 1913.
[9] *Ibid.*
[10] R. S. Baker and W. E. Dodd (eds.), *The New Democracy,* I, 32.

leadership as a partisan working exclusively through
the Democratic membership and congressional ma-
chinery. There were signs during the months before
his inauguration that he would attempt to construct a
new coalition, but for a number of reasons Wilson decided to remain what he always thought the President
should be—a prime minister, the leader of his party, the
responsible spokesman for a legislative program. He
was able to establish such leadership, incidentally, without wholly alienating the insurgents and independents;
and when he reconstructed the Democratic program in
1916, he was able to draw most of the independents into
the Democratic ranks.

He took party leadership simply by asserting it boldly.
In Trenton, before his inauguration, he assumed control
by conferring in person and by correspondence with
committee chairmen and Democratic leaders in Congress over the general structure of a legislative program.
In Washington, he gave close attention to the minutiae
of legislation, conferred frequently at the Capitol and
the White House, brought Congressional and cabinet
leaders together, mediated when it seemed that fundamental differences between conservatives and progressives might disrupt the Democratic ranks, and, when
necessary, cracked the patronage whip and used the
House and Senate Democratic caucuses to force rebels
into line.

He quickly won control through the sheer force of
personality and by using all the inherent powers of the
party leader. "I claim no superior attributes of mind or
decision over you or over any man in my party," he
would tell a protesting congressman; "but you overlook
the fact that I have been designated by the people to
hold this office and be the official head of this nation. I

am simply the instrument of the people for carrying
out their desires as I understand them. It is my best
judgment that this thing should be done in this way,
and you should acquiesce in that judgment; for I must
bear the burden of the responsibility to the people, and
not you; and I have no desire to divide that responsibility or shift it. I have given this matter careful consideration. This procedure seems right to me. I ask you
to adopt my plan. If you do not I am perfectly willing
to submit both my plan and yours to the people and
abide by their decision; but until the people relieve me
of my responsibilities those responsibilities are para-
mount, and I must insist on my own conception of my
duty."[11]

Although he could threaten and use the patronage as
ruthlessly as any President in our history to compel
obedience, Wilson preferred to win the support of congressmen by appealing to their reason and their sense
of national duty. "We always come away feeling that
we have been convinced, not by Mr. Wilson—certainly
not driven or bossed by him—but with the feeling that
we are all—President, Congress, and people—in the presence of an irresistible situation," a friendly congressman
once explained. "Here are the facts, he says; here are
the principles, here are our obligations as Democrats.
What are we going to do about it? He has a curious way
of making one feel that he, along with all of us, is perfectly helpless before the facts in the case."[12]

In one sense this description of Wilson's method is
accurate. On numerous critical occasions, as during the
discussions over the Federal Reserve bill in 1913 or the

[11] Samuel G. Blythe, "Wilson in Washington," *Saturday Evening Post,* CLXXXVI (November 8, 1913), 8.
[12] Ray S. Baker, "Wilson," *Collier's,* LVIII (October 7, 1916), 6.

preparedness measures in 1916, he compromised important points to gain a larger goal and won his objectives by leading instead of by driving. And yet we cannot escape the conclusion that Wilson was also the master in the showdown, determined and able to bend the Democrats in Congress to his personal will, able even to effect sudden and violent shifts in policy without the previous knowledge and consent of his party associates.

One observer stated the matter shrewdly: "He is agreeable, mild-mannered, pleasant, even solicitous about it all; but . . . he is firmly and entirely the leader, and insists upon complete recognition as such. He smiles when he tells a man to do a thing, but that smile does not decrease or soften the imperativeness of the order. He is a polite but not an easy boss. . . . He is the top, the middle and the bottom of it [all]. There is not an atom of divided responsibility. He has accepted every issue as his, has formulated every policy as his, and is insisting—and with success—on strict adherence to his plans. The Democratic party revolves round him. He is the center of it; the biggest Democrat in the country—the leader and the chief."[13]

Such aggressive boldness worked, among other reasons, because few congressmen and senators dared to challenge Wilson. Because there was no congressional machine capable of resistance, congressmen and senators stood alone in opposition to the man who had completely fused the powers of party leader and Chief Executive. As a perceptive English observer noted, they were, besides, "conscious of an intellectual inferiority, of a narrower point of view, of the limitations in their knowledge, of less elevated purposes and motives, of an

[13] S. G. Blythe, "Wilson in Washington," *loc. cit.*, p. 8.

almost entire ignorance as to how things will strike him."[14] Finally, most Democratic congressmen and senators, even many of the Southern veterans, depended upon Wilsonian approval and Federal patronage for their political existence. They usually had no alternative but to follow the President, even when he insisted upon policies that they thought were catastrophic.

But whether Wilson achieved results by leading or by driving is at this point irrelevant. The important fact is that Woodrow Wilson had substantially transformed the American presidency by the end of his tenure. When Franklin D. Roosevelt later recovered the full powers of national and party leadership for the presidency, some critics accused him of acting in a unique and revolutionary way to subvert the Constitution and establish a personal dictatorship. Actually, he was only following the example of the President under whom he had served for eight years as Assistant Secretary of the Navy.

So much for Wilson's philosophy and methods of leadership and the way in which he expanded the powers of the presidency. What does the historian have to say about the impact of his leadership on the long future of the American political economy?

It is easy to exaggerate the influence of great men and to forget that the origins of ideas, movements, and events are exceedingly complex. But even after one admits that Woodrow Wilson was more the product than the molder of his age, there still remains the fact that by the common agreement of historians he has a secure place among the first rank of Presidents of the United States. This is true in so far as he won this place in history through

[14] Sydney Brooks in the London *Daily Chronicle*, March 4, 1914.

domestic achievement, not because he was a pioneer in the progressive movement like Bryan, La Follette, or Theodore Roosevelt, but rather because he brought the progressive movement to its first culmination on the national level. The interesting fact about the reforms of the first Wilson administration was not that Wilson originated them. Indeed, the plans and proposals that he advocated had long been championed by other men in both parties. The interesting fact was the impact of Wilson's own leadership in the form of definite legislative achievement, and the way in which he adapted his program in response to the political realities and necessities of his time.

Wilson began his presidential term with simple objectives and a program designed merely to destroy the influence of big business in Washington and to unleash the economic energies of the American people through a return to a modified system of *laissez faire*. The first phase of his program, the New Freedom, which lasted from 1913 to about the end of 1914, substantially achieved the goals that Wilson had outlined in his first inaugural address. There was the Underwood Tariff Act of 1913, which imposed a degree of foreign competition upon American manufacturers and reflected the Wilsonian ideal of legislation in behalf of all the people rather than for special interests. There was the Federal Reserve Act of 1913, which made possible the mobilization of the banking resources of the country and the issuance of a volume of currency adjusted to the fluctuating needs of the American economy. There were the Clayton Antitrust Act and the Federal Trade Commission Act of 1914, which reflected the Wilsonian demand for a strengthening of the antitrust laws in order to prevent the growth of monopoly through the destruction of competition.

These were all Wilsonian measures, in the sense that in them the President synthesized contemporary political demands in legislative form and pushed them through Congress, often by the sheer force of personal will. And yet even more significant than Wilson's formulation and sponsorship of this New Freedom legislation was the way in which he adapted his program to meet the criticisms of a large group of advanced progressives, both Democrats and Republicans, who demanded the adoption of a more aggressive program of Federal assistance to farmers, workers, and the disadvantaged classes.

Indeed, the pressures for a bolder program of Federal control began at the outset of Wilson's first term and notably affected even the New Freedom phase of Wilsonian reform. Under steady progressive hammering, for example, Wilson approved changes in the Federal Reserve bill that made it serviceable to farmers as well as to businessmen and provided for a measure of public control of the new banking system. In response to severe progressive criticism, moreover, Wilson enlarged his antitrust program to include provision for a Federal Trade Commission empowered to use direct action to prevent destructive competition.

The impact of Wilson's leadership on Federal legislative policies was greatest and most significant, however, after the end of the New Freedom phase. To state the matter briefly, beginning in the early months of 1916 Wilson abandoned the ideal of reform through a program of modified *laissez faire* and espoused virtually all the advanced progressive demands for Federal social and economic intervention that he had earlier opposed or refused to support—a Federal rural credits system, a

Federal child labor bill, a tariff adjusted to the needs of the business community rather than for sheer revenue, a significant increase in the income tax and a Federal inheritance tax, a measure establishing the eight-hour day for interstate railroad workers, and other such measures. That the President succeeded in putting this program across in 1916 was perhaps the clearest evidence of his control of his party, for the Democrats who in the past had championed state rights and fought the extension of the Federal authority now joined progressive Republicans and Wilson in enacting the most significant program of Federal social and economic legislation in American history to that time.

Largely through Wilson's leadership, therefore, the United States for the first time attempted squarely to confront the enormous domestic problems of the twentieth century. The program begun by Theodore Roosevelt and aimed at building public administrative power to offset the aggregations of private power came to its first culmination under Wilsonian auspices and to an even fuller fruition after 1932. If this is true, then historians a century hence will probably describe the Wilson era as the time when the American people through their leaders found the first, though incomplete and imperfect, answers to the question of how to bring a dynamic, growing, and competitive economy under effective social control. This was no mean accomplishment, and we conclude by remembering that this thing happened, in part, because Woodrow Wilson lived.

From Isolation to Mediation

*Archibald Cary Coolidge Professor of History,
Harvard University*

It is most appropriate that we should gather here this
evening to observe the centennial anniversary of Woodrow Wilson's birth. For Bryn Mawr was, as you know,
the scene of his first academic assignment. During the
three years of his professorship here he meditated on
many aspects of American life and arrived at some of
the views upon which he was later to base his policies.
I am greatly honored by the invitation to address you
on certain aspects of those policies as they touched international affairs and as they affected the relationship of
the United States to the rest of the world. I will not
attempt in the time allotted me to cover the complicated and controversial subject of Mr. Wilson's foreign
policy in any detailed or systematic way, but will con-
fine myself to the evaluation of certain features of that
policy as it emerged during the period of our neutrality
in the first World War and as it evolved during our
participation in the hostilities and the peace settlements.
I am sure that you do not expect of me, as an historian,
an uncritical panegyric, but rather a judicious assessment of the aims and achievements of a man who, hardly

more than a generation ago, was hailed by the peoples of a war-torn world as the harbinger of a new and better international order and who is still revered as one of the truly noble figures of modern times.

It seems to me that for us and for the whole contemporary world what is important about Woodrow Wilson's foreign policy is its bearing on the eternal question of war and peace, for our reconsideration of which the first World War and the Paris Peace Conference provide the necessary backdrop.

At the very outset one is bound to be struck by the fact that Mr. Wilson, though an authority on American history and a leading educator, had at best but a superficial knowledge of and nothing more than a general interest in foreign affairs when he succeeded to the presidency in 1913. He had, it is true, already recognized that the passing of the frontier in the 1890's was bound to make the conditions of life in the United States more difficult, and that in the future the country would have to abandon its cherished isolation in order to seek in the larger world arena the needed outlets for the expansive impulses which he regarded as the natural expression of mature national strength. But he had not followed up this general proposition with any specific suggestions or programs. In fact, his interest remained concentrated on domestic issues. From time to time he might visit the British Isles, but on only one occasion, in 1903, did he stray as far afield as France and Italy. His papers and records contain nothing to suggest close study of particular foreign issues or even much preoccupation with the broader aspects of international relations.

Like most Americans of his time, Mr. Wilson considered the United States unique among the nations—a land of liberty, equality and opportunity whose greatness depended not so much upon its material wealth as upon its spiritual strength. During the period of its growth the country had, he believed, rightly held aloof from the sordid rivalries and everlasting conflicts of Europe. But now, in the days of its splendid maturity, the United States had a sacred mission to provide leadership to other nations. It should stand as the champion of freedom, justice, and peace, and should be prepared to serve selflessly the interests of humanity. The President's response to the crisis of July, 1914, which was to eventuate in the Great War, was to express publicly the hope that the world would turn to the United States for "those moral inspirations which lie at the basis of all freedom" (Fourth of July Address, 1914).[1] When, presently, the storm broke over Europe, Mr. Wilson, like most of his countrymen, regarded this newest and most terrible conflict merely as the latest manifestation of the crass materialism, the ruthless ambition, the political immorality and the baleful power politics which had always sullied the history of the Old World. It looked like "a natural raking-out of the pent-up jealousies and rivalries of the complicated politics of Europe," he remarked on a later occasion.[2]

Mr. Wilson knew little and evidently cared less about the origins and causes of the cataclysm. After two years of life-and-death struggle he could still state publicly that he and his countrymen were not concerned to search for the obscure foundations from which the stupendous flood had burst.[3] He had always hated war and

[1] Harley Notter, *The Origins of the Foreign Policy of Woodrow Wilson* (Baltimore, 1937), 307.

[2] Quoted by George F. Kennan, *American Diplomacy, 1900–1950* (Chicago, 1951), 63.

[3] Address to the League to Enforce Peace, May 27, 1916.

regarded it as a barbarous method of settling international issues. The conflict in Europe, he once remarked, was like "a drunken brawl in a public house."[4] It was a most disgusting spectacle, but as between the antagonists his sympathies were decidedly with Britain and France. He was easily persuaded that Germany had been guilty of aggressive trade policies and that German philosophy was essentially selfish and devoid of spirituality. On the other hand, Britain and France were democracies, defending liberty and popular government against the forces of German militarism and autocracy. Was not France the victim of attack, and was not Britain fighting in fulfillment of a moral obligation to defend Belgian neutrality? Such observations and queries were not very profound and hardly exhausted the crucial problem of responsibility for the Great War. But they evidently satisfied the President, who seems never to have been troubled by serious doubts about these matters.

Colonel Edward M. House, Mr. Wilson's intimate adviser, as well as prominent American diplomats like Walter Hines Page and James W. Gerard held the same views but were more sophisticated and articulate in their partisanship. From the outset they were convinced that the Germans, if victorious, would eventually move against Latin America or even the United States itself. It was therefore in the American interest to support the Allied powers in every way possible, if need be even by force of arms. They expounded this thesis to the President time and again, but Mr. Wilson was reluctant to believe in the threat to American security. He agreed that the victory of Prussian militarism and autocracy would bode ill for the future of democracy, but he never

[4] Stephen Gwynn, *The Letters and Friendships of Sir Cecil Spring-Rice* (Boston, 1929), II, 356.

really despaired of the ultimate victory of Britain and France.

This was in general the sentiment of the country also. Even those who recognized the importance for American security of the maintenance of the British position did not regard the defeat of the Allies as imminent or even probable. It is easy, therefore, to understand the absence of any marked sentiment for American intervention in the war. Neutrality was the natural expression of the country's traditional attachment to isolation. For the President, however, neutrality soon came to take on a special significance: it meant to him the maintenance of the strictest impartiality so that, when the time was ripe, the United States might serve as mediator, to bring the antagonists together and ensure the conclusion of a just peace. In short the war, hateful though it was, might provide a unique opportunity for that selfless service to humanity of which Mr. Wilson dreamed. America was, he felt, peculiarly fitted for the role of mediator, for it was "the mediating nation of the world," as he declared in April, 1915. "We are compounded of the nations of the world. . . . We are, therefore, able to understand all nations. . . . It is in this sense that I mean that America is a mediating Nation."[5] Already he envisaged himself attending the eventual peace conference as the exponent of America's spiritual leadership, already he was interesting himself in projects for an association of nations to safeguard the world against further armed conflict.

In my opinion it was this basic attitude toward the European War that determined the President's entire

[5] Address to the Associated Press, April 20, 1915, quoted by Robert E. Osgood, *Ideals and Self-Interest in American Foreign Relations* (Chicago, 1953), 179.

policy during the period of American neutrality. I do not mean to belittle the gravity or importance of his long disputes with Britain as well as with Germany over the well-worn issue of freedom of the seas. Neither do I mean to ignore the thesis, so popular in the period between the two World Wars, that the President and the American people were duped by British propaganda and victimized by powerful munitions and banking interests who, in their anxiety to forestall the defeat of Britain and France and protect the huge American investment in those countries, finally engineered the intervention of the United States just as the Allied cause was beginning to fail. These matters are certainly of great interest and importance, but they have been so thoroughly and judiciously treated by Professor Charles Seymour in his essays on *American Neutrality, 1914–1917* (New Haven, 1935) and by other writers that, so far as I can see, little if anything remains to be said. My time being limited, I have elected to analyze and evaluate certain less familiar aspects of American policy.

It is important for my argument to realize that Mr. Wilson, though he regarded the British and French as the defenders of liberty and democracy against militarism and autocracy, as nations standing "with their backs to the wall, fighting wild beasts,"[6] did not for that reason intend to show partiality in the conduct of American relations with the belligerents. Some critics have taxed him with unwarranted tolerance of British violations of the freedom of the seas. But it should be noted that, however reluctant to hamper the British war effort, Mr. Wilson was frequently irritated and at times positively infuriated by British disregard of international law. Per-

[6] Mr. Wilson's remarks to his cabinet in April, 1915, quoted by Charles C. Tansill, *America Goes to War* (Boston, 1938), 205.

sonally, I do not agree with those who contend that his numerous notes of protest to London were mere window dressing. On the contrary, I think he intended them as detailed specifications of American claims to be presented when the war was over.

On the assumption, then, that Mr. Wilson meant to hold the British as well as the Germans accountable for their methods of warfare, it was nevertheless an inescapable fact that British violations of international law involved only property rights, whereas Germany's unrestricted submarine warfare inevitably entailed the loss of human lives. It has often been argued, with undeniable cogency, that the Germans, subjected to rigid blockade and exposed to possible starvation, could hardly be blamed for resorting to any weapon in their effort to break the grip of British seapower. The submarine was a new weapon, for which existing international law made no provision. The rules of cruiser warfare were hardly adequate, for a submarine attempting to stop and search a merchant ship on the high seas ran the risk of being immediately rammed or sunk by gunfire. The armament which merchant ships were permitted to carry for defense against cruisers could be used with great effect for offensive action against submarines. The submarine commander had therefore but little choice. Unable to bring his prize to port, he had to sink it. In the interest of his own and his crew's safety, he had to sink it with little or no warning.

Secretary of State Bryan, Senator William J. Stone, and many others argued from these simple facts that the only way to prevent loss of American lives on belligerent ships was to forbid American citizens from traveling on them and to prohibit American-flag ships from entering declared war zones. But the rights of neutrals were clear and the President refused to surrender them. There-upon Mr. Bryan resigned, but Senator Stone and some of his colleagues pressed the issue. Whatever the legal rights of Americans, Stone contended, it was "fool-hardiness amounting to a sort of moral treason against the Republic," for citizens to risk their lives on armed belligerent ships. To this President Wilson replied in a well-known letter that "no group of nations has the right, while the war is in progress, to alter or disregard the principles which all nations have agreed upon in mitigation of the horrors and sufferings of war, and if the clear rights of American citizens should very un-happily be abridged or denied by any such action, we should, it seems to me, have in honor no choice as to what our course should be. For my own part, I cannot consent to any abridgment of the rights of American citizens in any respect. The honor and self-respect of the nation is involved. . . . Once accept a single abate-ment of right and many other humiliations would cer-tainly follow, and the whole fine fabric of international law might crumble under our hands piece by piece." The rights of neutrals, he held, were among the "inalienable rights" of mankind. The United States was therefore contending for nothing less high and sacred than the rights of humanity. Refusing all compromise, then, the President notified Berlin that the Imperial Government would be held "strictly accountable" for the loss of American lives. Following the sinking of the *Sussex* (March 24, 1916) he threatened American intervention to force the Germans to stop sinking merchant ships by submarine without prior warning and without due pro-vision for the safety of passengers and crew.

The President's attitude on the submarine issue was determined in part by his larger aims. Over and over

again in his so-called preparedness speeches of early
1916, he stressed the fact that Americans were "a body of
idealists, much more ready to lay down their lives for a
thought than for a dollar"; that they were the "trustees
of the moral judgment of the world," and that other nations looked to them "to keep even the balance of the
whole world's thought." There was, therefore, a price
too high to pay even for peace and that was the price of
self-respect, of duties abdicated, of glorious opportunities neglected. Everything points to the conclusion that
to his own mind the President was defending the right
as against all violators. In the case of the Germans, however, human rights as well as neutral rights were involved. When finally he felt obliged to ask Congress to
declare war on Germany, it was primarily because the
Imperial Government by overt acts had demonstrated
its readiness to override international law in a desperate
drive for victory.

The President has often been criticized for having
pitched American policy on the high plane of general
principles. He should have seen, it is said, that Germany
threatened the security of the sea lanes between the
United States and Britain, that our national interest required the continued existence of Britain and that it
therefore forbade the domination of Europe by an un-
friendly Germany. For that reason if for no other he
should much sooner have committed the United States
to active participation in the war.

As a matter of fact this facet of the problem was obvious to discerning minds in both official and unofficial
circles, and I find it difficult to believe that the President
was entirely unaware of it. But, as I have said before,
hardly anyone, not even the exponents of a "realistic"
policy, considered the threat of German victory im-

minent. The position of the Allies, militarily and economically, was believed to be better than we now know it to have been, and the whole trend of public thought was so averse to intervention for anything but the highest motives that even so uncompromising a realist as Theodore Roosevelt felt impelled to explain the entry of the country into the war in terms of the struggle for democracy against autocracy, for liberty against tyranny, and for right against wrong.[7] Analyzing the popular attitude in April, 1917, the British agent, Sir William Wiseman, stated in a report approved by the President: "It is important to realize that the American people do not consider themselves in any danger from the Central Powers. It is true that many of their statesmen foresee the danger of a German triumph, but the majority of the people are still very remote from the war. They believe they are fighting for the cause of Democracy and not to save themselves."[8]

Since the national security did not appear to require American intervention in the European War, the President felt entirely justified in maintaining neutrality, in acting as trustee of the moral judgment of the world and as defender of human rights. Above all, he was prepared and eager to provide good offices for the settlement of the conflict, as well as leadership in the organization of the world for peace.

This was the crux of his policy. It required, first and

[7] Article in the *Metropolitan Magazine,* July, 1917, quoted in Osgood, *op. cit.,* 151 ff.

[8] Charles Seymour, *The Intimate Papers of Colonel House* (Boston, 1928), III, 30; IV, 268. This estimate is generally supported by an analysis of American newspaper opinion. See Albert H. Buchanan, "American Editors Examine American War Aims and Plans in April, 1917" (*Pacific Historical Review,* IX, 1940, 253–265).

foremost, the maintenance of neutrality so as to retain the freedom of action necessary "to do the high thing we intend to do." The President hated war and would not resort to it except under extreme provocation: he was too proud to fight for anything but the highest values. "It would be a calamity to the world at large," he wrote Colonel House after the sinking of the *Arabic* (August 19, 1915), "if we should be drawn actively into the conflict and so deprived of all disinterested influence over the settlement." The same thought recurs much later, when the German decision to resort to unrestricted submarine warfare was already known in Washington and war had become all but inevitable. It would be a crime, said the President to Colonel House, to become involved in the conflict to such an extent that later the United States would be unable to save Europe. On the very eve of American intervention Mr. Wilson was still hoping that neutral powers would unite to support the American position and so induce the German government to reverse its fateful decision. Surely it is no exaggeration to say that one of the major objectives of neutrality was to fulfill the requirements of mediation.

Hardly less prominent in the President's mind was the concept of peace without victory. Obviously, if either side were to win a decisive victory, it would not desire nor would it accept American mediation. The chances were great that total victory would produce a harsh, punitive peace. "Victory," said the President in his great programmatic address to the Senate on January 22, 1917, "would mean peace forced upon the loser, a victor's terms imposed upon the vanquished. It would be accepted in humiliation, under duress, at an intolerable sacrifice, and would have a sting, a resentment, a bitter memory upon which terms of peace would rest, not permanently, but only as upon quicksand." He saw all too clearly that upon such a foundation it would be impossible to erect a new international order. He therefore clung to the principle of a compromise settlement, concluded between equals.

It was not the President's idea, however, that the United States should take a hand in drafting the terms of the European peace settlement. It might aid in bringing the antagonists together, but the latter would then have to find their own settlement of the issues in dispute. The interest of the United States would be solely in the establishment of a new concert of power, a universal association of nations to guarantee the settlement, if it were a just one, and to provide for common action against any nation which in future should resort to war. Such at least was Mr. Wilson's initial conception, as he expounded it to the League to Enforce Peace on May 27, 1916. Before long, however, he came to see that the United States, if it were to undertake large responsibilities for the preservation of world peace, would of necessity be deeply interested in the nature and even the details of the peace settlement. The treaties ending the war, he told the Senate on January 22, 1917, "must embody terms which will create a peace that is worth preserving, a peace that will serve the several interests and immediate aims of the nations engaged." Since a decisive victory held little promise of such a settlement, he laid increasing emphasis on the need for a compromise peace, that is, a peace without victory. Furthermore, he began to advance the thesis that the new international system should be set up first of all, so that the erstwhile belligerents, their security guaranteed by

the concert of nations, would have no further need to
seek security through the imposition of punitive measures.

The evolution of the President's thinking no doubt
reflected his disillusioning experiences as a would-be
peacemaker. In the initial days of the war he had ten-
dered his good offices in an effort to end hostilities. Both
sides had declined, and soon after, at the end of September, 1914, the British rejected an American suggestion
that discussions looking toward peace be held by the
ambassadors of the belligerent powers in Washington.
On this and on subsequent occasions the Germans expressed a readiness to engage in negotiations. In fact,
they at times urged the President to mediate. But they
did so only when the military situation was in their
favor. Postwar studies of German objectives and above
all the extremely harsh terms imposed on Bolshevik
Russia in the Treaty of Brest-Litovsk (March, 1918)
leave no shadow of doubt that the Germans until the
time of their imminent military defeat were willing to
discuss peace only on their own terms.

It was perhaps natural that the President should look
primarily to the British for co-operation in bringing the
war to an end and establishing a new and better world
order. Common traditions, common outlook, and common language should all have facilitated understanding.
But the British were in this respect to prove a grave
disappointment. They showed little if any desire for
guidance or salvation. Sir Edward Grey, the Foreign
Secretary, was an early convert to the idea of a League of
Nations and expressed readiness to make peace as soon
as there were real promise of a durable settlement. He
expressed doubt whether it would be either feasible or
desirable to crush Germany, and averred that Britain

and France, if victorious, would negotiate a fair and reasonable settlement with their fallen foe. But only if and when a military victory proved impossible would Grey and his countrymen welcome friendly American mediation.[9]

Sir Edward was, so it seems, just about as anxious to circumvent mediation as the President was to secure its acceptance. Yet the British Foreign Secretary was probably more favorably disposed toward the American policy than most of his cabinet colleagues or than the British public at large. Most newspapers were violently opposed to neutral mediation. A few Liberal organs like the *Economist,* the *Nation,* the *Contemporary* and the *Manchester Guardian* stood with Grey as advocates of a reasonable peace and at times even expressed a desire for American mediation. But the other newspapers and journals denounced and abused them for their pains. Mr. Asquith, the Liberal Prime Minister, had sounded the keynote of British policy when, on November 9, 1914, he declared in his Guildhall speech: "We shall not sheathe the sword . . . until the military domination of Prussia is fully and finally destroyed."[10]

It must have been disheartening to the President and Colonel House to have their high-minded proposals meet so cool a reception. But they considered the question of peace much too important to be shelved. In January, 1915, Colonel House went to London as Mr. Wilson's personal representative to see if he could discover, in intimate discussions, whether there was a possibility of initiating peace talks. But again British leaders, from

[9] George M. Trevelyan, *Grey of Fallodon* (New York, 1937), 310 ff., 314.

[10] See particularly Armin Rappaport, *The British Press and Wilsonian Neutrality* (Stanford, 1951), 102 ff.

King George to Sir Edward Grey, left their visitor in no
doubt that peace efforts were useless and that American
mediation was not wanted. Grey, however, made every
effort to convince his visitor that Britain shared the
President's high ideal of a new world order in which
war would be outlawed and disarmament would become possible. The important thing, he argued, was that
America should commit itself to participate fully in future world affairs.[11]

It would be both interesting and instructive to follow
in detail the ensuing phases of this problem. I have time,
however, only to touch upon the main developments
and to underline the more important features. House's
second wartime visit to Europe, in the early months of
1916, satisfied him that there was no disposition in
Berlin to make concessions and that in London too,
"peace discussions at this time would be about as popular . . . as the coronation of the Kaiser in Westminster
Abbey."[12] The British desired the United States to
enter the war, but only on the issue of German submarine warfare, so that the Allies might remain free
with respect to future peace terms.[13] So anxious was
House to stage a peace conference and so intent were
the British not to offend or estrange the Americans, that
Grey eventually agreed to a memorandum submitted
by House with the approval of President Wilson.

This Grey-House Memorandum was a truly remark-
able document, for it specified that, on hearing from
Britain and France that the moment was opportune,
President Wilson should demand the convocation of a

[11] Seymour, *The Intimate Papers of Colonel House,* I, 385–390;
Trevelyan, *op. cit.,* 315.
[12] Seymour, *Intimate Papers,* II, 184.
[13] *Ibid.,* II, 173.

conference to put an end to the war. Should the Allies accept and the Germans refuse, the United States would "probably" enter the war against Germany. It was House's opinion that if such a conference met, it would establish peace on terms "not unfavourable" to the Allies; if it failed to secure peace because of German unreasonableness, the United States would ("probably" was added by Mr. Wilson) leave the conference as a belligerent on the side of the Allies.[14]

If this loosely worded agreement meant anything, it meant that President Wilson and Colonel House were so eager to end the war and establish the new world order that they were prepared to act in collusion with the Allies to compel the Germans to attend a peace conference and accept terms "not unfavourable" to the Allies, on pain of having the United States enter the war against them. The British, who were as much opposed to American mediation as ever, were not called upon for any commitment. Indeed, the whole scheme was to go into operation only when they gave the word. In other words, they could appeal to the President if their situation became positively desperate, and could rely upon the United States to ensure them "not unfavourable" terms.

As a matter of fact the British never took advantage of what on its face appears to have been a most attractive offer. Possibly they doubted whether the Congress would in any contingency vote for war. Possibly they had but a poor opinion of the military contribution the United States could make within any reasonable period.

[14] Text in Seymour, *Intimate Papers,* II, 201. See also the illuminating discussion, based in part on unpublished materials, in Arthur S. Link, *Woodrow Wilson and the Progressive Era* (New York, 1954), VIII.

More likely, however, they still regarded American mediation as the least desirable solution of their problem. British opinion was still firmly opposed to all outside interference and equally set against a negotiated peace.

The plan embodied in the Grey-House Memorandum was the brain child of Colonel House rather than of the President, and we may assume, I think, that Mr. Wilson went along with it only for want of some better method of attaining his objective before it was too late. Still he was disappointed by the obstinate refusal of the British to accept American direction. In a public address on May 27, 1916, he announced the readiness of the United States to become a partner in a League of Nations and outlined his ideas as to the nature of such an association. In no uncertain terms he bade farewell to isolation: "We are participants, whether we would or not, in the life of the world. . . . The interests of all nations are our own also. We are partners with the rest. What affects mankind is inevitably our affair as well as the affairs of the nations of Europe and Asia."

Yet even this epoch-making pronouncement was vehemently attacked by the British press. Mr. Wilson, in speaking of the war, had remarked: "With its causes and objects we are not concerned." To the British, even to those in high circles, these words revealed a lack of understanding not only of the origins, but also of the objectives of the struggle. Some even suggested that the President had fallen a victim to German "peace claptrap."[15]

It is easy to understand the "emotional reaction" of the President, to which Mr. Seymour several times refers in his work on the House papers. Mr. Wilson was

[15] Seymour, *Intimate Papers*, II, chap. 10; Rappaport: *The British Press and Wilsonian Neutrality*, 111 ff.

disgusted as well as discouraged. It was at this time that he spoke of the war as "a drunken brawl in a public house," and privately referred to the British leaders as "poor boobs." On another occasion he told House that he could see no justification for helping the Allies "to destroy Germany politically and economically, so that France and Russia might divide the dictatorship of the Continent and Great Britain be rid of German naval and commercial competition."[16]

Months passed by without noticeable change in the British attitude. On September 16, 1916, the *Spectator* denounced all ideas of a "great, flat, flabby, overgrown international Pow-wow . . ."; and presently Mr. Lloyd George declared that "the fight must be to the finish—to a knock-out"; intervention by other powers in behalf of peace, he added, would not be tolerated. These uncompromising words cannot be dismissed as an irresponsible outburst, for they were followed up by equally stiff statements from the Prime Minister and the Foreign Secretary (October 11, 23). Perhaps the clearest and most succinct definition of the British position appeared in a memorandum prepared by Sir Edward Grey for the Cabinet at the end of November: "As long as the naval and military authorities believe that Germany can be defeated and satisfactory terms of peace can eventually be dictated to her, peace is premature, and to contemplate it is to betray the interests of this country and of the Allies."[17]

During the closing months of 1916 the German gov-

[16] Quoted by N. C. Peterson, *Propaganda for War* (Norman, 1939), 285, from the House papers at Yale. See also Link, *Woodrow Wilson and the Progressive Era,* 219 ff., for the President's reaction.

[17] Trevelyan, *Grey of Fallodon,* 323.

ernment was doing its utmost to induce the President to arrange discussions for peace. The German military situation was still favorable, but it was becoming increasingly clear that a decisive German victory could be won only through the reintroduction of unrestricted submarine warfare. The High Command realized that such a move would bring the United States into the war against Germany, but was perfectly confident that Britain could be brought to its knees long before American aid could become effectual. The civil authorities, however, remained opposed to the submarine program and hoped that peace could be attained on acceptable terms before the final, fateful decision was made.

The President, on his part, firmly refused to make any further moves until after the November election, the result of which he could interpret as an expression of public support for his foreign policy. But the situation in the Allied countries at the end of 1916 was anything but propitious for mediation. Anglo-American relations had reached their nadir as a result of British interference with American trade and mail, and the announced British intention of fighting on to a knockout spelled the doom of any further American effort to mediate. Yet the President felt that he must act to forestall further bloodshed such as had marked the offensive on the Somme, and to ensure a new order of international affairs before either side was completely exhausted.

His initial thought seems to have been simply to demand that the belligerents cease hostilities on pain of American intervention. But this variant on Colonel House's earlier program depended so greatly on the sheer military power by which it could be backed that it must have seemed to the President impracticable. Eventually, on December 18, 1916, he simply called on both sides for a statement of the terms on which they would be prepared to conclude the war and of the arrangements they would deem satisfactory as a guarantee against its renewal or the kindling of a similar conflict in the future. He disclaimed any effort at mediation and, though he offered his services if desired, he insisted that he had no wish to determine the method or the instrumentality. He warned, however, that the United States, while not at liberty to suggest terms, had a genuine interest in the conclusion of peace, lest its position as a neutral become intolerable. Furthermore: "If the contest must continue to proceed toward undefined ends by slow attrition until one group of belligerents or the other is exhausted; if million after million of human lives must continue to be offered up until on the one side or the other there are no more to offer; if resentments must be kindled that can never cool and despairs engendered from which there can be no recovery, hopes of peace and of the willing concert of free people will be rendered vain and idle."

The President's note was less pretentious than his earlier proposals. He seems to have had real difficulty in formulating his suggestion and evidently hastened its completion because the German government itself had a week before proposed a conference of the belligerents. Mr. Wilson was much concerned lest the British, by turning down the German proposal, should bang the door on peace. Perhaps he was also disturbed by the possibility, however slight, that the belligerents might make peace without American participation and without providing guarantees for the preservation of peace in the future.

In his haste Mr. Wilson again allowed an infelicitous statement to slip into his note: "The objects which the

statesmen of the belligerents on both sides have in mind
in this war are virtually the same as stated in general
terms to their own people and to the world." The ensuing passage shows clearly that by this the President
meant simply that the belligerents had stated their aims
in general terms and that it might be well now to present specifications. But the first part of the questionable
sentence was bitterly attacked in the Allied countries.
King George is said to have wept as he expressed his
surprise and depression,[18] while nothing would deter the
new Prime Minister, Mr. Lloyd George, from airing his
feelings in a public speech (December 19) in reply to
the German overture. In no uncertain terms he declared that peace could be obtained only on the basis of
"complete restitution, full reparation, and effectual
guarantees." What this signified was spelled out in
greater detail in the official British reply to the President's note (January 10, 1917) which left no doubt that
the Allies meant to fight on until victory made possible
the imposition of Draconian terms. Small comfort was
to be derived from the statement that, while the Allies
desired to shield Europe from the covetous brutality of
Prussian militarism, the extermination and the political
disappearance of the German peoples had never formed
part of their designs.

Despite the fact that the German government had
expressed its preference for direct negotiations with its
enemies, and despite the uncompromising attitude of
the London government, the President decided to press
on with his program, for he knew that important decisions were in prospect on the German side and that
time was probably running out. In one of his great addresses to the Senate (January 22, 1917) he asserted that

[18] Seymour, *Intimate Papers,* II, 407.

in making his proposal for a statement of peace terms he was speaking "on behalf of humanity and of the rights of all neutral nations." It was true, he continued, that the United States would have no voice in establishing the concrete terms of peace, but it would certainly have a voice in deciding whether or not peace should be made lasting by the guarantees of a universal covenant, the need for which all parties recognized. It was not enough to say, as statesmen of both belligerent groups had said, that it was no part of their purpose to crush their antagonists. A durable peace could not be based on a victor's terms, but could only be a "peace without victory." "Only a peace between equals can last. Only a peace the very principle of which is equality and a common participation in a common benefit. The right state of mind, the right feeling between nations, is as necessary for a lasting peace as is the just settlement of vexed questions of territory or of racial and national allegiance."

Once again the British found in the President's words grounds for protest, this time with reference to the phrase "peace without victory." But on this occasion their indignation was superfluous, for within a week the President was notified of the German decision to resume unrestricted submarine warfare on February 1. Berlin's repudiation of its earlier engagements made the severance of diplomatic relations inevitable, yet Mr. Wilson still hoped that a common front of neutral states could be formed and that the Imperial government might give way to combined pressure. At all events he would await overt acts on the part of the Germans before asking Congress to declare war.

The sinking of several American ships and the resulting loss of life left the President no choice but to accept the German challenge. Still, in explaining the situation to Congress (April 2, 1917), he made no effort to conceal his disappointment and grief. The German government, by resorting to a form of warfare which he described as "warfare against mankind," had compelled the United States to take up arms "to vindicate the principles of peace and justice in the life of the world as against selfish and autocratic power. . . ." Despite the latest disheartening developments, however, his own thought, he said, had not been driven from its habitual and normal course. He did not blame the German people, for whom he felt nothing but sympathy and friendship. Not they, but their ruthless and irresponsible rulers had brought the world to this pass. Clearly no autocratic government could be trusted to keep its faith. If there were ever to be a concert for peace, it could only be a partnership of democratic nations. The world, therefore, had to be made safe for democracy.

It is impossible to read the historical record for this period without sensing what a blow to Mr. Wilson's dearest hopes was the German proclamation of unrestricted submarine warfare. He felt that it had forced him to take his country into the war at the very time when the prospect for peace negotiations and American mediation seemed at long last to be growing brighter. Now the whole picture had changed: the United States as a party at interest could no longer serve as impartial mediator, and there was real danger that an Allied victory, to which the United States was now bound to contribute, would eventuate in a punitive peace which, in turn, would make impossible a new world order of justice and co-operation.

America's entry into the Great War obliged the President, therefore, to undertake a thorough reconsideration of his policy. The ensuing changes I should like to examine in my second lecture, but in closing tonight I trust you will permit me to restate the leading theme of my argument.

President Wilson has been taken to task for his failure to recognize the requirements of American security and for basing his foreign policy on moral principles and the idea of selfless service to mankind rather than on the simple demands of national interest. Though this thesis has been seriously overworked, it certainly has some validity. I have tried to explain it by recalling the traditional American attitude of aloofness and superiority to the sordid politics of Europe. Woodrow Wilson set his countrymen a higher goal and a nobler mission than any they had yet envisaged. Everything we can learn of public opinion at that time indicates that the American people gladly shared his aspirations and loyally supported his policies.

Furthermore, it appeared to the country, as it did to him, that the United States, having no territorial or other selfish aims and being in no way threatened by developments in Europe, had a real obligation to further its high ideals. Those who hold that in the interests of national security the President should at an early date have taken the country into the war against Germany overlook the fact that relatively few people at that time recognized the eventual threat involved in a German victory. Even the historians, whom the general public seems to think can look forward as well as backward, were for the most part blind. Long after the war many of them still argued that American intervention was a mistake, no matter what the shape of things to come in Europe.[19]

[19] Edward M. Earle, "A Half-Century of American Foreign Policy: Our Stake in Europe, 1898–1914" (*Political Science Quarterly,* LXIV, 1949, 168–188).

It was just because the President believed that the United States had nothing to fear and had no axe to grind that he hoped to mediate, to aid in arranging a just peace and above all to provide leadership in organizing a new international order that would prevent war in the future. He had dreamed of something like this since early manhood. To play the role of peacemaker would have been infinitely gratifying to him. But to qualify for the part he had to stand immovable by the international law on which he hoped to build the new order. Furthermore, he had to keep his country out of the conflict if at all possible. And finally, he had to induce and if necessary force the belligerents to accept neutral mediation and abandon the idea of a fight to the knockout. To me it is clear that Woodrow Wilson, for all his lack of knowledge and interest in concrete European issues, saw more clearly than most that a decisive victory would almost inevitably produce a punitive peace and that such a peace could not possibly serve as the foundation for a society of nations. This, I submit, was statesmanship of a high order.

Woodrow Wilson: The Test of War

Eric F. Goldman

Professor of History, Princeton University

The day Woodrow Wilson called upon Congress to declare war against Germany, he rode away from the thunderous applause and sat pale and silent in the Cabinet Room of the White House. At long last he spoke to his secretary, Joseph Tumulty. "Think what it was they were applauding," the President said. "My message today was a message of death for our young men. How strange it seems to applaud that."

Wilson went on to speak of how he had tried to avoid war, had seen it surely coming, and had pursued a patient policy so that public opinion would move with him. "There is but one course now left open to us," he added firmly. "Our consciences are clear, and we must prepare for the inevitable—a fight to the end."

Still the President kept on talking, taut, troubled talk. The administration was sure to be "misconstrued." A "storm of criticism and ridicule" lay ahead. Long days of "tragedy and heartaches" were at hand. Finally, Tumulty remembered, Wilson "drew his handkerchief from his pocket, wiped away great tears that stood in his eyes, and then laying his head on the Cabinet table, sobbed as if he had been a child."

The grim business of presidential war leadership was on, grimmer still because of the complex, high-tensioned nature of this particular President. Day after day Woodrow Wilson sat in the big lonely office on the south side of the White House, keeping a fierce grip on his nerves, managing most of the time to preserve an outward appearance of calm and graciousness. Mrs. Wilson and the White House physician helped; they saw to it that he spent a morning on the golf course, an afternoon on horseback or taking a long automobile ride, an evening at the theatre. The President's conscience-lashed sense of responsibility did the rest. He had decided that America belonged in this war; he would spare nothing of himself to see it through.

Once in a while utter weariness overcame him. He would tell a cabinet meeting at the end of a harrowing two hours that he must ask to be relieved of departmental matters; he simply "was unable to think longer." Once in a while the nerves would fray into a querulous letter or a snappish reply to one of the endless stream of men who came to tell him how to win the war. Often Wilson made his decisions in a torture of doubt. "How much more troubled, how much more unsure I am," he wrote an intimate, "than people believe me to be." But then the decision would come, the snappishness and the weariness passed, and Wilson was the war President of the public view, the tall, dignified figure, the long face graven, the jaw jutting out in assurance and decisiveness.

To Congress Wilson was the whiplash of the New Freedom days, his driving habits now intensified by the emergency. "In wartime," Wilson said, "it is the duty of the President to lead, ever lead. I will not shirk my duty." The Congressional opposition stirred to set up a

Joint Committee on the Conduct of the War, which would have provided a means of checking Presidential power. Wilson threw every possible ounce of White House pressure against the proposal and smashed it. Along the way Congress fumed and stormed at this or that aspect of the way affairs were being run. The Administration often took steps to meet the criticism but Wilson never conceded in the slightest that a fundamental responsibility for conducting the war could be placed anywhere except in the White House. Any man representing the White House was sure of the President's most potent support against Congressional or public opinion.

To Congress, no Wilson subordinate was more provocative than George Creel. He was brilliant, quick-tongued, and imperious. He was, moreover, head of the most controversial of the war agencies, the Committee on Public Information which handled the propaganda. At a high point in the tension of the war, Creel went to New York to make a speech and during the question period he was asked: "Do you think all members of Congress have 'loyal hearts?' "

Creel shifted impatiently on his feet and then placed both of them squarely in his mouth. "I won't explore into the hearts of Congressmen," he said. "I do not like slumming."

Immediately the House and Senate rang with cries for the resignation of Creel. He apologized but the uproar went on, including demands that Creel be hauled before the House of Representatives and cited for contempt. One afternoon Creel's telephone rang and he found the President on the other end of the wire.

Wilson said: "I trust you are not worrying over the antics of the House?"

"Well, sir," Creel sighed, "I can't say I'm very happy."

"I was afraid," the President continued, "that you might be taking it seriously, and I called up to say that if they do cite you for contempt, I'll be only too glad to act as your counsel."

A short while later a delegation of senators visited Wilson to enforce the protests by threatening to cut off the $50,000,000 emergency presidential fund from which Creel's organization was paid. Wilson entered the room where the senators were gathered, bowed formally, and listened politely to their grievance. Then he said: "Gentlemen, when I think of the manner in which Mr. Creel has been maligned and persecuted, I think it is a very human thing for him to have said. Good morning."

To Wilson the heart of the war problem was the necessity for a never-ending newness of approach. This conflict was different from any the country had ever known, the President kept telling the nation. It was America's first total war, and total war meant meshing the population's whole life—its manpower, its factories, its farms, its thinking—into one gigantic machine of force. Early in the war, Wilson spoke out his deep conviction in an off-the-record speech to the officers of the Atlantic Fleet. "The point that is constantly in my mind," he said, "is this: This is an unprecedented war. . . . We have got to throw tradition to the wind. [Since] . . . nothing that I say here will be repeated I am going to say this: Every time we have suggested anything to the British Admiralty the reply has come back that virtually amounted to this, that it had never been done that way, and I felt like saying: 'Well, nothing was ever done so systematically as nothing is being done now.' Therefore, I should like to see something unusual happen, something that was never done before; and inasmuch as the things that are being done to you were never done before, don't you think it is worth while to try something that was never done before against those who are doing them to you? There is no other way to win, and the whole principle of this war is the kind of thing that ought to hearten and stimulate America. . . . America is the prize amateur nation of the world. Germany is the prize professional nation of the world. Now when it comes to doing new things and doing them well, I will back the amateur against the professional every time, because the professional does it out of the book and the amateur does it with his eyes open upon a new world and with a new set of circumstances. He knows so little about it that he is fool enough to try to do the right thing. . . . That is the kind of folk we are. We get tired of the old ways and covet the new ones."

The new ways came with machine-gun force and rapidity. When Congress voted war in April, 1917, the United States was woefully unprepared to fight a war, total or otherwise. The pressure of war and of Wilson's ineluctable leadership turned one extraordinary novelty after another into fact. The idea of a national selective service act horrified millions, including the Speaker of the House, Champ Clark, who bluntly declared: "In Missouri we see little difference between a conscript and a convict." The Selective Service Bill quickly became law. Two decades of progressive agitation had made rule by businessmen a subject of the darkest suspicion to a large part of the country. The War Industries Board, headed by a multimillionaire businessman, Bernard Baruch, and staffed largely by dollar-a-year corporation executives, was soon exercising near-dictatorial powers over the American economy. For decades the

word "propaganda" had called up a sinister picture of
Old World machinations, if it called up anything at all.
Within months George Creel's Committee on Public
Information was flooding the United States, not to
speak of the world, with a literature that was to reach
close to the hundred million pieces in number.

Next to his drive for new instrumentalities to meet
the new situation, Wilson was most concerned with the
equitable distribution of sacrifice. He was not a historian for nothing; he knew the bonanza which war can
offer to profiteers. Having taken over the philosophy of
the progressive reform movement which was sweeping
America in the early 1900's, the President was the more
anxious that his war administration should avoid economic or social favoritism. In the midst of some of his
worst military worries, he paused to encourage protec-
tions against child labor. He stepped hard on a proposal
to draft strikers. He kept urging state governments to
watch moves to undermine social legislation. And more
than once he publicly tongue-lashed intransigent em-
ployers in a way that had them crying "dictator" and
"Bolshevik."

Wilson did not prevent gigantic profiteering. In the
twenty months of fighting at least two thousand mil-
lionaires suddenly appeared on the scene, and other parts
of the population managed to acquire succulent slices
of the wartime pie. Yet three drastic moves of the administration severely leveled profit and sacrifice. In an
era when the whole idea of income taxes was startlingly
new, considerable progressive taxes were placed on in-
comes and inheritances, and burdensome levies were
made upon the excess profits of corporations and part-
nerships. In spite of the fact that many ingenious
schemes were devised by lawyers and accountants for

absorbing the shock, including the highly effective device of issuing new stock in lieu of dividends, a weight of taxation that would have seemed revolutionary in the age of Lincoln fell upon the rich. Speaking of the upper range of the tax structure, the leading authority of the day, Professor Edwin R. A. Seligman, declared: "This is the high water mark thus far reached in the history of taxation. Never before in the history of civilization has an attempt been made to take as much as two-thirds of a man's income by taxation."

Other important Administration policies showed the same attitude. Numerous contracts were made on the basis of the new idea of cost plus a commission—a device which discouraged fraud and made it much easier for labor to get increases in wages commensurate with the mounting inflation. A major portion of the war expenses was met by interest-bearing securities that were issued on terms of a severity which would have horrified Civil War bankers. Only the first of these issues, the smallest in amount, carried the exemption from taxation which had been customary in national loans. What's more, the bonds were not sold through syndicates on a generous commission basis but over the counter with a specific compensation for financiers.

In many ways the Wilson war leadership on the home front was superb. It permitted far less profiteering and corruption than the Lincoln period, showed far more imagination than the Franklin Roosevelt years. In many ways it was bold, inventive, idealistic, and effective.

In many ways—that phrase is the key one, for interlaced through all the hard-driving idealism was something quite different, incongruously, shockingly different. Hatred, a bitter, unreasoning, self-destructive rancor, ran unchecked through the country. Civil liberties were being twisted, narrowed, virtually abolished in the traditional American meaning of the word. Woodrow Wilson occasionally intervened in a minor case, occasionally he spoke for reason within the Administration councils, but for the most part he raised not a finger. By the middle of the war he would not take a stand even on the silliest forms of the hysteria. The conductor of the Philadelphia Orchestra wrote him and asked whether he thought Bach and Beethoven should be removed from programs. The President instructed Tumulty to reply with a monumental shilly-shally. "Won't you write a kind letter . . . ," Wilson directed, "suggesting this to him: 'It is not a question which can be decided on its merits, but only by the feelings and present thoughts of the audiences to whom the Philadelphia Orchestra and the other orchestras of the country play.' "

The anti-German furor mounted until the utterly ridiculous and the utterly savage were pathetically intertwined. Restaurants changed the name of sauerkraut to "Liberty cabbage," and reports flowed in of German-American children beaten up in the schools. Universities solemnly banned instruction in the German language and from Outagamie County, Wisconsin, came the sworn statement of a German-American, John Deml. Late one Sunday night a crowd of men came pounding at Deml's door, demanding that he sign up for Liberty bonds. Deml told the crowd he had already done his share by buying $450 in bonds, and then "all at one time . . . ," as Deml told the story, "[they] closed in on me like a vise; some grabbing my fingers or wrist, others my legs, and several of them were shouting, holding a paper before me, 'Sign up.' I said, 'I will not sign up at this time of night.' Then a man shouted, 'Get the rope!' The first I knew was when the rope was about my neck and around my body under my arms. Someone then gave a sharp jerk at the rope and forced me to my hands and knees; at the same time some of them jumped on my back, and while bent over someone struck me in the face, making me bleed; then a man . . . said, 'Boys, you are going too far. . . .' "

Early in the war, the Administration and Congress rushed through sweeping legislation dealing with espionage, sedition, and trading with the enemy, and many local governments followed suit. These laws created a situation in which virtually any criticism of the Wilson administration could be ruled illegal. As the country's most distinguished authority on civil liberties, Zechariah Chafee of Harvard, has pointed out, it became criminal to advocate still heavier taxation instead of bond issues or to argue that a referendum should have preceded our declaration of war.

The administration of the laws was no less oppressive. A nationwide spy system was created. According to incontestable evidence, "tools" were planted among organizations and were instructed to incite them to unlawful acts. The meeting places of these associations were raided without proper warrant, property was destroyed, papers seized, innocent bystanders beaten, and persons guilty of no discernible offense sent to jail, subjected to police torture, held without bail, and released without recourse.

Not untypically, Wilson's postmaster general, A. R. Burleson, denied mailing privileges to the antiwar radical journal, the *Masses,* on the ground that it contained treasonable passages, and then refused to name the offending passages when the publisher offered to delete the material. Federal Judge Learned Hand overruled

Burleson, and the postmaster general promptly found another technique of suppression. The *Masses* had missed an issue because of the original suppression. Hence, Burleson decreed, it was no longer a regularly issued periodical and was not eligible for second-class privileges. The postmaster general cracked down on an issue of a single-tax magazine called *The Public,* which urged that more money should be raised by taxes and less by loans. He suppressed Thorstein Veblen's book *Imperial Germany and the Industrial Revolution,* which the President's own Committee on Public Information had recommended. He contemplated moving against the *New Republic* magazine, as Walter Lippman has bitterly recalled, "for advocating a Wilson-type peace in the mad days of 1918."

Many prosecuting and judicial officers operated in the same spirit. The persons indicted or imprisoned included a woman who had received a Red Cross solicitor in what was called a "hostile" manner; a tailor who had written a letter to the *Kansas City Star* charging wartime profiteering; and an editor who printed the statement: "We must make the world safe for democracy even if we have to 'bean' the Goddess of Liberty to do it." A Californian went to jail for laughing at rookies drilling on San Francisco's Presidio, a New Yorker served ninety days for spitting on the sidewalk near some Italian officers. In Los Angeles a movie-maker was sentenced to ten years and a five-thousand-dollar fine for producing a film about the American Revolution. The film, the judge said, "tended to make us a little bit slack in our loyalty to Great Britain in this great emergency."

Outside the government, the contagion of suppression spread rapidly. Radical labor leaders were tarred and feathered, ministers were unfrocked for emphasizing the Sermon on the Mount, clubs expelled members who questioned the omniscience of the administration, college professors were dismissed or bludgeoned into resigning for pacifist leanings or for ardent prowar statements that also criticized the home front. Both the unofficial and the official hysteria fell more and more under the control of conservatives, who were just as interested in silencing reform agitation as they were in suppressing friends of Germany. Sometimes the witch-hunt appeared primarily a reform-hunt. Cases were numerous like that of the dismissal of Professor J. McKeen Cattell, a well-known psychologist, by the Columbia board of trustees. Cattell had opposed American entrance into the war, but he was doing nothing that could remotely obstruct the war effort. On the contrary, his son, with the father's approval, had volunteered for combat service, and the psychologist himself was at work on plans to guide the War Department in its selection of aviators. But Cattell was a long-time critic of the Columbia board of trustees, which at that time exercised flagrantly autocratic control over the faculty and was bitterly reactionary. Twice before the United States entered the war, the trustees tried to maneuver Cattell's dismissal and retreated only when the faculty sharply protested. Now, Cattell could charge, "the trustees have hid behind the flag to assassinate."

Not only was hysteria sweeping the country. The administration was doing little to give the public any real understanding of the way that it saw the war and the peace. Wilson's private papers reveal a powerful mind, operating with more than a little sense of reality about the coming problems. His public addresses talked the language of the primer. The gigantic opinion-molding being done by George Creel's Committee on Public Information had an identical cast. From all of this the ordinary citizen could derive only a picture of the most illusionary simplicity. A war to make the world safe for democracy . . . a war to end wars . . . a peace without victory. No one, not even a man of Woodrow Wilson's semantic magic, can sloganize reality. The truth, unfortunately, requires a few sentences or even a whole paragraph.

Supporters of the President, ardent friends of his ideals, fought hard to change the situation, but in vain. One of them, taking the strongest possible measure to try to call attention to what was happening, has left a poignant memory of the tragedy. A week after the dismissal of Cattell at Columbia, Professor Charles Beard finished his customary afternoon lecture, then added: "This is my last lecture in Columbia University. I have handed in my resignation this afternoon to take effect at 9 A.M. I thank you."

The next day his militant letter of resignation appeared in the principal metropolitan newspapers. The Cattell dismissal could not be permitted to go unrebuked, Beard declared. It was bad enough to force conformity on men in the most ordinary times. "But these are not ordinary times. We are in the midst of a great war and we stand on the threshold of an era which will call for all the emancipated thinking that America can command." The country desperately needed arguments addressed to "reason and understanding and humaneness. . . . Such arguments can only come from men whose independence is beyond all doubt."

Independent, emancipated, humane thinking—here was the heart of what was needed to bring American support to Woodrow Wilson's vision of a new world. Professor Langer's essays discuss foreign policy with distinguished authority and it would be foolish to trespass in his domain. In seeking the meaning of Wilson's activities at home, however, it is necessary to stress that foreign policy was Wilson's climactic concern and that his program in international affairs essentially called for an adventurous, moderate, flexible, nonvindictive approach. What was happening in American public opinion directly undercut support for such a program. The assaults on the reform-minded groups in the United States stifled the influence of the most understanding and ardent friends of Wilsonianism. The frenzied hatred of Germany brought an enormous pressure for a saber-rattling, old-fashioned, vindictive peace. The kind of understanding of the war and the peace that had been achieved by sloganizing, by reaching a least common denominator of ignorance and oversimplification, hardly prepared minds for the intricacies of building a world order. The whole atmosphere of truculent conservatism was the worst possible climate for a presidential plan which, after all, called for a very brave and a very new brave new world.

Why did Wilson do it? Why did he make no real effort to halt, and why did he actually aid, the development of a public opinion which would destroy his most cherished objectives?

The question is a more arresting one because Wilson himself had seen with extraordinary prescience what war could do to public opinion. The night before he mounted the rostrum of Congress to call for a declaration of war, Wilson had sat talking with an intimate friend, Frank Cobb of the *New York World,* and the newspaperman has left us a description of the President's startling premonition. "He said," Cobb reported the President's conversation, that "war would overturn the world we had known. . . . It would mean we should lose our heads along with the rest and stop weighing right and wrong. It would mean that a majority of people in this hemisphere would go war-mad, quit thinking and devote their energies to destruction. . . . It means an attempt to reconstruct a peace time civilization with war standards.

"When a war got going, it was just war and there weren't two kinds of it. Once lead this people into war and they'll forget there ever was such a thing as tolerance. . . . The spirit of ruthless brutality will enter into the very fibre of our national life, infecting Congress, the courts, the policemen on the beat, the man in the street." Conformity would be the only virtue, the President concluded grimly.

In seeking to understand why Wilson did so little to check a danger which he saw so clearly, part of the answer must be found in the mind and personality of this intricate human being. Despite the torture Wilson went through in making decisions, the decision was not between shades. There was only black and white, Good and Evil, the godly and the ungodly. A good deal of the kind of opinion that was being crushed in the United States during 1917–18 was tinctured with criticism of Wilson's administration or even outright opposition to the war. He had decided that the war, and the way he was conducting it, were Good; that was that. Woodrow Wilson had a habit of confusing himself with God and when critics tried to straighten out the confusion, it was not too surprising that the President was ready to have them treated as if they were engaged in desecration.

Moreover, Wilson's own prewar forebodings seem to have created a degree of fatalism in his reaction to the hysteria. "We couldn't fight Germany and maintain the ideas that all thinking men shared . . .," he had told Cobb. "It would be too much for us." Too much for us —this does not sound like the stern Covenanter of the iron faith. But there has been, I suspect, an overdegree of pigeonholing Wilson as the supremely confident idealist and certainly some of his reaction to the frenzied swirl of public opinion showed a sense of helplessness that fits no simple stereotype.

Whatever the role of Wilson's personal qualities, they are not the whole story or perhaps even the most important part of the story. Speaking to Sir Cecil Spring-Rice in early 1918, he expressed his conviction that the chief function of a wartime President was to prevent "civil discord." The problem which "any American President had to face," he said, "was in the main a psychological one. He had to gauge public opinion. He had to take the course which commended itself to the great majority. . . . It was not so much a question of what was the right thing to do from the abstract viewpoint as what was the possible thing to do, from the point of view of the popular mind." The chief function of a wartime President, in short, was to preserve unity.

This concern over unity was directly connected with Wilson's reluctance to take positive steps to check the hysteria. At times one can see him starting to move, then drawing back; if he stepped athwart so powerful a current of opinion, would he not divide the country in a serious way? Less plainly but no less surely, one can see the concern over unity halting Wilson from spelling out to the public some of the richer, more intricate bases of his thinking about foreign policy. Americans could agree on slogans, that democracy was good and militarism was bad, that it would be fine to have something called a

world league. They would hardly have been as much in
agreement on what Wilson had in the deeper recesses
of his mind—that, to quote the President, "the isolation-
ism of the United States is at an end, not because we
chose to go into the politics of the world but because by
the sheer genius of our people and the growth of our
power we have become a determining factor in the history of mankind."

Another element in the situation was still less a product exclusively of the President's own qualities. Throughout the history of the United States, and never more so
than in the progressive years when Wilson came to political maturity, a potent idea has run through American
thinking. For millions the point has been so deeply believed that it has amounted to a credo, a mystique. Ordinary people are good, the credo runs. In the long run,
they are wise. They may have their aberrations; they
may be misled. But before long they will adjust themselves, get to the heart of the matter, and come up with
the decent and sensible solution.

Woodrow Wilson was a quite unusual American in
many ways, but he was of the purest stock in his total,
unqualified, near-mystical faith in ordinary people.
Were there signs that America was turning against his
ideals? "Not America," Wilson corrected visitors, "but
partisan malcontents. Watch the people assert themselves." Was the public pitifully informed to make the
kind of decisions he would call upon it to make? "Never
distrust the wisdom of the simple man," Wilson said.
"He will make the sound decisions."

Near the end of the war Harold Ickes, then a youth-
ful pro-Wilson idealist, went to the President with a
passionate protest. "Can't you see what is building out

there—hatred, foolhardiness, reaction—everything that abhors your aims?"

The President's tone was patient. "You are young, Ickes. When you are as old as I, and have seen as much of this country in operation, you will know that the people take hold and take hold well and take hold never far in the future."

For Woodrow Wilson the future had come and it had gone.

The war hurtled to a close. Wilson's own thinking had never been more free-wheeling, more bold, more pragmatic. He talked privately of the League of Nations "not as a way of abolishing power politics but of restraining it," of the troubles between nationalities in Europe, of the connections between domestic and foreign politics. He sat conversing with his brother-in-law, Stockton Axson, and his thoughts roamed far and challengingly. "The next President," Wilson said, "will have to be able to think in terms of the whole world. He must be internationally minded. Now as a matter of fact, the only really internationally minded people are the labor people. They are in touch with world movements.

"The world is going to change radically, and I am satisfied that many governments will have to do many things which are now left to individuals and corporations. I am satisfied for instance that many governments will have to take over all the great natural resources . . . the water power, the coal mines, all the oil fields, etc. . . . It is because I am not a socialist that I say these things. I think the only way these countries can prevent communism is by some such action as that."

To his friends the President might speak hard, bold,

highly suggestive words, the kind of words that made
sense out of Wilsonian programs for a sweepingly different world. Out to the people of the United States,
from the President and the Committee on War Information, went only more of the thin, arid, abstract
phrases.

Up from the public, more violently than ever, came
the snarls of reaction, hatred, jingoism. The President
stirred not a whit.

The blows fell fast. As Germany was surrendering,
the Congressional election of 1918 came on, and the
public slapped Wilson hard by returning a Republican
House and Senate. Another few months and the Lodge
Round Robin Senate resolution was cutting further
ground from under the President. Another short period
and the League of Nations itself was reeling under the
blows of senators who echoed the dervish of ignorance
and hate in the country.

Woodrow Wilson took to the road. He would go to
the ordinary people; he would set off their natural good
sense and idealism. Out across the country the President
swung, some 8,000 miles, out to Seattle and then back
toward the East. Now Wilson was using every weapon
in his arsenal. At Omaha he said: "I can predict with
absolute certainty that within another generation there
will be another World War if the nations of the world
do not concert the methods by which to prevent it." At
San Diego he declared: "I do not hesitate to say that the
war we have just been through . . . is not to be compared with the war we would have to face the next
time." At St. Louis he said: "I would like to get together
the boys who fought in the war and I would stand before them and say: 'Boys, I told you before you went

across the seas that this was a war against wars . . . but
I am obliged to come to you in mortification and shame
and say I have not been able to fulfill the promise. You
are betrayed. . . .' "

It was late, very late, even for such powerful weapons.
As the President was nearing Colorado his head was
racked with pains. At Pueblo the paralysis struck, and
the train was rushed back to Washington with drawn
blinds. Before and after Wilson's stroke, the Senate,
amply fortified by the jungle public opinion created
during the war, went on tearing Wilsonianism to pieces.

For Woodrow Wilson, now there were only the bitter,
broken last years—the last years and the legacy to his
nation which the centennial year of 1956 has commem-
orated. Like everything else about this extraordinary
figure, the heritage to us is not simple. No President
has ever summoned this nation to a nobler standard.
None has given it more electrifying leadership. None has
presided over so tragic a debacle. Wilson's legacy as a
wartime leader, it would appear, is a brilliant glow of
idealism streaked with a dark warning—a warning of
special poignance for our generation which must fight
its own war, the cold war, with its own tortuous problem of somehow steering ideals, a faith in ordinary men,
and the importance of national unity through the calam-
itous dangers of an ill-informed and overwrought public
opinion.

Near the end of his years Woodrow Wilson spoke the
warning in one of those curious moods which sometimes
overcame his Covenanter certainties. In 1922, he sat in
his Washington home talking with a friend. In the middle of bitter, defiant assertions that the people, the plain
people, had always backed him in their heart of hearts,

the old man suddenly paused. He turned his gaunt face to gaze out the window for a long few moments and then he said quietly: "It is a terrible responsibility to lead a democracy in a war fought for an ideal. There is so much likelihood that the democracy will win the war and lose its soul."

Peace and the New World Order

WILLIAM L. LANGER

Archibald Cary Coolidge Professor of History,
Harvard University

The intervention of the United States in the first
World War, forced upon the government and the nation by Germany's resumption of unrestricted submarine warfare, entailed the abandonment of the policy
by which President Wilson had set so great store. As a
party at interest he could no longer hope to serve as impartial mediator to induce or coerce the belligerents to
cease hostilities before either side were decisively defeated, and to ensure that the peace settlement was suffi-
ciently reasonable and just to provide an adequate base
for an international organization to prevent the recur-
rence of conflict.

Once the United States had entered the lists against
Germany it had, of course, no alternative but to strive
for victory. To the President this meant first and foremost the destruction of Prussian autocracy. The Imperial government's violation of its earlier promises had
reinforced his conviction that "no autocratic government should be trusted to keep faith with or observe its
covenants," and that, therefore, "a steadfast concert for
peace can never be maintained except by a partnership

of democratic nations."[1] This idea, which goes back at least to the eighteenth century, rests on the proposition that the average man has so much to lose, or at any rate so much to risk by war, and so little to gain, that, given a chance to express himself, he will choose peace. "I sometimes think," said the President in an address at Milwaukee (January 31, 1916) "that it is true that no people ever went to war with another people. Governments have gone to war with one another. Peoples, so far as I remember, have not. . . ." It therefore followed that "democracy is the best preventive of such jealousies and suspicions and secret intrigues as produce wars among nations where small groups control rather than the great body of public opinion."[2] The great objective must be to make the world safe for democracy. Through the depth of his conviction and the eloquence of his oratory the President united the country in pursuit of this end and imbued it with idealistic fervor to such an extent that the war on the American side has often been called a "crusade."

Mr. Wilson realized that the country, because of its traditional isolation and its strong sense of distinctness, was opposed to a formal alliance with foreign powers and he therefore merely "associated" the United States with the Allied nations. But he probably had additional reasons for avoiding too intimate a connection. He had, for example, grave suspicions of Allied war aims and evidently still hoped that, when the time for peacemaking arrived, he could keep aloof from the wrangling and throw the weight of the United States into the scales on

[1] Address to Congress, April 2, 1917.
[2] Interview with the *Washington Post* (November 5, 1916), quoted by Harley Notter, *The Origins of the Foreign Policy of Woodrow Wilson* (Baltimore, 1937), 568–569.

the side of justice. In proclaiming a crusade against militarism and autocracy he was on absolutely safe ground, because the Allies themselves had proclaimed this war aim at the very beginning of the conflict and even Mr. Wilson's most uncompromising opponents, Theodore Roosevelt and Senator Henry Cabot Lodge, had espoused the same cause.[3] But beyond the sublime heights of generality stretched a valley of doubt. The Allied reply to the President's note of December 18, 1916, had set forth conditions for peace that could be realized only through total victory. Furthermore, it was clear that the Western powers meant to attack the crucial problem of world organization for peace only after they had provided for their security by drastically reducing, if not destroying the military and economic power of their enemy.

This program ran counter to the President's deepest convictions, for he saw at the end of the conflict (if I may borrow a sentence from Charles Seymour) "not so much military triumph and chastisement of an enemy, as the vision of a new international structure, in the creation of which the United States might take the lead."[4] It has been suggested that under these circumstances Mr. Wilson should have concluded an agreement as to peace terms before taking the country into the war. Since,

[3] See Roosevelt's article in the *Metropolitan Magazine*, July, 1917, as quoted in Robert E. Osgood, *Ideals and Self Interest in America's Foreign Relations* (Chicago, 1953), 151 ff. On Lodge's position see John A. Garraty, *Henry Cabot Lodge* (New York, 1953), 333. That American newspapers in general supported this thesis is shown by the analysis of Albert R. Buchanan, "American Editors Examine American War Aims and Plans in April, 1917" (*Pacific Historical Review*, IX, 1940, 253–265).

[4] Charles Seymour, *The Intimate Papers of Colonel House*, (Boston, 1928), III, 2.

however, the United States was forced into the war, he was hardly in a position to lay down conditions for American cooperation.

Besides, he had not yet worked out his specifications for a just and durable peace. He had not concerned himself at all with the territorial or other problems of Europe, partly because he expected the Europeans to settle these problems for themselves and partly because he considered specific questions secondary in importance to the organization of the world for peace.

Strangely enough, he had not progressed beyond general principles even with respect to the future League of Nations. Colonel House kept him informed of British thought and writing on international organization, and he was certainly posted on the activities of the American League to Enforce Peace. But he steadfastly refused to consider concrete proposals for the constitution of the prospective world organization. He wanted, so he said, to avoid premature discussion and controversy. Furthermore, he was convinced that institutions, to be healthy, must grow naturally. "We must *begin* with solemn covenants, governing mutual guarantees of political independence and territorial integrity (if the final territorial agreements of the peace conference are fair and satisfactory and *ought* to be perpetuated), but the method of carrying those mutual pledges out should be left to develop of itself, case by case."[5]

In April, 1917, Lord Balfour, the new British Foreign Secretary, came to the United States to discuss Allied needs. Balfour agreed with Colonel House that a discussion of war aims should be avoided: "If the Allies begin to discuss terms among themselves, they will soon

[5] Seymour, *Intimate Papers*, IV, 4, 16, 49.

hate one another worse than they do Germany. . . ."[6]
But it seemed altogether impolitic not to inform the
President of the secret treaties which the Allied powers
had concluded among themselves and which formed the
basis for their proposed territorial reshaping of Europe,
the Near East and East Asia. Colonel House was disgusted with some of the provisions of these treaties and
we must assume that the President, too, was disagree-
ably impressed by them, though it is at least possible
that he failed to grasp all the implications of these un-
edifying transactions. For the moment at any rate he
made no issue of the matter and evidently consoled himself with the thought that when the time came the
United States could take its stand. In July, 1917, he
wrote House: "England and France have not the same
views with regard to peace that we have by any means.
When the war is over, we can force them to our way of
thinking, because by that time they will among other
things be financially in our hands."[7] To me this is a
most revealing remark, and I have no doubt that Mr.
Wilson, when in September, 1917, he asked Colonel
House to assemble a group of experts to study the peace
aims of the various powers and the way in which the
United States might respond to them, meant this move
as the first step toward securing Allied acceptance of
the American program.[8]

[6] Letter of House to the President, April 22, 1917, in Seymour,
Intimate Papers, III, 37 ff.

[7] Seymour, *Intimate Papers,* III, 51, 147. The full text, as I
quote it, is given only in Seymour's biography of Wilson in the
Dictionary of American Biography (New York, 1936), XX, 352–
368.

[8] Seymour, *Intimate Papers,* III, 169; Sidney E. Mezes, "The
Inquiry," in Edward M. House and Charles Seymour, *What
Really Happened at Paris* (New York, 1921) chap. 1.

The attempt to forestall dispute over war aims became hopeless when the Bolsheviks, having seized power
in Russia (November, 1917), promptly published the
secret treaties so as to discredit the tsarist regime and ex-
pose the iniquities of bourgeois imperialism. The Western powers thought it imperative to counter these reve-
lations and if possible to deflate Bolshevik proposals for
peace on the basis of no annexations and no indemnities.
In addition, however, President Wilson wanted to serve
notice on the Allied powers that there must be a revision
in a liberal sense of the war aims reflected in the secret
treaties. Through Colonel House and Sir William Wiseman he tried to persuade London and Paris to join in a
manifesto of liberal war aims. But Mr. Lloyd George,
when sounded out by Wiseman, rejected the idea "with
angry emphasis."[9] The President thereupon decided to
act on his own and called upon his group of experts—
the Inquiry—to draft the basic terms of an acceptable
peace.

On January 5, 1918, Mr. Lloyd George, fairly well
posted on what the President proposed to say and no
doubt intent upon having the first word, expounded in
a public address a program of war aims much more moderate than the one he had advanced a year earlier. Many
of his points were quite consonant with those the President was about to propose, though with regard to a possible organization to enforce peace the Prime Minister
reiterated his conviction that this project could be un-
dertaken only after the re-establishment of the sanctity
of treaties and after "a territorial settlement based on
the right of self-determination."

Despite the fact that Mr. Lloyd George had taken

[9] Seymour, *Intimate Papers*, III, 278 ff., 322 ff.; Arthur Willert,
The Road to Safety (London, 1952), 134.

much of the wind out of his sails, President Wilson decided not to abandon his own pronouncement. On January 8, 1918, he submitted his famous Fourteen Points to Congress and to the world. Several of them were statements of general principles, but most of them dealt with concrete issues of a territorial nature. Thus Mr. Wilson for the first time indicated American readiness to assume some responsibility for the specific terms of peace, as contrasted with plans for world organization. It should be noted, however, that the Fourteen Points were all couched in broad, rather vague terms, well designed to serve their propaganda purpose, but hardly suited to the negotiations of which, in the sequel, they were to become the basis.

The Fourteen Points, although not officially recognized by the Allied Governments, proved one of the most effective subjects of propaganda in modern history. While giving new hope and confidence to liberal elements throughout the world, they encouraged the enemy to hope for a reasonable settlement and so reinforced the growing agitation for peace in Germany. Hitler is reputed to have later complained: "For four years our enemies tried to defeat us and they finally had to get an American medicine man to find the formula that deceived the German people."[10]

By September, 1918, the German military machine was beginning to stall, and the President concluded that it was high time to restate the American position, as well as to induce the Allied governments to subscribe formally to his program. In conversation with his secretary, Joseph Tumulty, he remarked: "What I greatly fear, now that the end seems inevitable, is that we shall

[10] John L. Snell, "American Rhetoric Goes to War" (*The Historian*, XIV, 1952, 191–208).

go back to the old days of alliances and competing arma-
ments and land-grabbing. We must see to it, therefore,
that there is not another Alsace-Lorraine, and that when
peace finally comes, it shall be a permanent and a lasting
peace. We must now serve notice on everybody that our
aims and purposes are not selfish."[11]

This the President did in his address at the Metropolitan Opera House opening the Liberty Loan Drive
(September 27, 1918). His words were "brutally frank,"
as he felt they must be, with friends as with foes: "If it
be indeed and in truth the common object of the Governments associated against Germany and of the nations
whom they govern, as I believe it to be, to achieve by
the coming settlements a secure and lasting peace, it
will be necessary that all who sit down at the peace table
shall come ready and willing to pay the price, the only
price, that will procure it; and ready and willing also to
create in some virile fashion the only instrumentality by
which it can be made certain that the agreements of the
peace will be honored and fulfilled. That price is impartial justice in every item of the settlement, no matter
whose interest is crossed; and not only impartial justice,
but also the satisfaction of the several peoples whose for-
tunes are dealt with. That indispensable instrumentality
is a League of Nations formed under covenants that will
be efficacious. . . . And, as I see it, the constitution of
that League of Nations and the clear definition of its objects must be a part, is in a sense the most essential part
of the peace settlement itself." The United States, he
continued, was prepared to assume its full share of responsibility for the maintenance of the peace settlement,
provided it were based on certain principles. Of these

[11] Joseph Tumulty, *Woodrow Wilson as I Know Him* (New
York, 1921), 301–302.

the first specified that "the impartial justice meted out must involve no discrimination between those to whom we wish to be just and those to whom we do not wish to be just. It must be a justice that plays no favorites and knows no standard but the equal rights of the several peoples concerned." In conclusion the President called on Allied statesmen to tell him plainly if he was mistaken in his interpretation of the issues or of the means by which they might be solved.

There was hardly time for allied statesmen to reply, for in early October the German government appealed to the President to invite the belligerents to enter upon peace negotiations on the basis of the Fourteen Points and to conclude an armistice at once. It must have seemed to the President that the golden moment had after all arrived—that, despite America's involvement in the war, he was to have the chance to mediate the peace. In order to ensure the success of his program he decided to risk the wrath of the Allied governments by conducting the initial negotiations without even consulting them. His inclination was to make a soft reply to the German note, but before he could do so he found himself exposed to a powerful and to him no doubt quite unexpected outburst of public feeling among his own countrymen. The German note was popularly thought a trap to catch the President in a negotiated peace. The public clearly expected him to reject it and to prosecute the war to a crushing military victory—to unconditional surrender. In the Senate voices were at once raised against all compromise. Even in the cabinet there were some who called for the "most stringent retribution."[12]

[12] Seymour, *Intimate Papers*, IV, 76 ff.; Earl S. Pomeroy, "Sentiment for a Strong Peace, 1917–1919" (*South Atlantic Quarterly*, XLIII, 1944, 325–337); Willert, *The Road to Safety*, 159.

From the diary entries of Colonel House we can sense the perplexity of the President when confronted with this upsurge of war madness. In the end he felt obliged to stiffen his reply to the Germans, demanding outright acceptance of the Fourteen Points and evacuation of invaded territories, and inquiring whether or not the German Chancellor spoke only for "the constituted authorities of the Empire." Eventually the German government accepted all his conditions, but the correspondence between Washington and Berlin was punctuated by an ever-growing agitation for war to the finish. Theodore Roosevelt and Senator Lodge led the campaign for unconditional surrender and a dictated peace. Resolutions against further negotiations were introduced in the Senate. In the country at large the National Security League, the League for National Unity and kindred organizations labored to the same end.[13]

The President was determined to stand firm against this savage vindictiveness. His position at this time is brilliantly reflected in the record of his luncheon conference on October 16 with Sir William Wiseman, who was about to leave for London to discuss with his government the acceptance of the Fourteen Points. Mr. Wilson remarked that, while he did not trust the German government, he could not slam the door on peace. In drafting terms it was necessary, he argued, to consider the condition of Germany: "If we humiliate the German people and drive them too far, we shall destroy all form of government, and Bolshevism will take its place. We ought not to grind them to powder or there will be

[13] Pomeroy, *loc. cit.;* Harry R. Rudin, *Armistice, 1918* (New Haven, 1944), 106, 124, 173–174; Karl Schriftgiesser, *The Gentleman from Massachusetts: Henry Cabot Lodge* (Boston, 1944), 296; John A. Garraty, *Henry Cabot Lodge* (New York, 1953), 340.

nothing to build up from." He was alarmed, he added, by popular demands for the devastation of Germany: "I want us on our side to end this war as finely as we began, and show the world that we are the better fellow." Furthermore, "he disliked the idea of settling peace terms without the enemies being present to state their case. It would give the impression of dividing the spoils among ourselves in advance." The same thing applied to the League of Nations: "Germany ought to be present when the League of Nations is constituted." The League, he reiterated, "should be the very centre of the Peace settlement, the pillars upon which the house will stand."[14]

Of the same tenor was the cable sent by the President to Colonel House after the latter's departure for Europe: "My deliberate judgment is that our whole weight should be thrown for an armistice which will not permit a renewal of hostilities by Germany, but which will be as moderate and reasonable as possible within that condition, because lately I am certain that too much severity on the part of the Allies will make a genuine peace settlement exceedingly difficult if not impossible."[15]

On October 23 the President at last communicated to the Allied governments his correspondence with Berlin, leaving them to decide whether or not they wished to conclude an armistice on the conditions accepted by the Germans. Thus far Allied statesmen had paid no particular attention to the Fourteen Points. Indeed, M.

[14] John L. Snell, "Wilson on Germany and the Fourteen Points" (*Journal of Modern History,* XXVI, 1954, 364–369). Parts of this report were published by Willert, *The Road to Safety,* 175. See also Seymour, *Intimate Papers,* IV, 83.

[15] Cable of October 29, 1918, in Seymour, *Intimate Papers,* IV, 110.

Clemenceau, the French premier, is said not even to have read them.[16] Furthermore, Allied leaders were not in a receptive mood. The British were indignant at the President's failure to consult them and fearful lest he be trapped by a wily enemy. They resented the American effort to foist the Fourteen Points on them.[17] But they were, with few exceptions, quite as ready as Mr. Wilson to conclude an armistice. The question for them was merely how severe the conditions could be made without too great risk of rejection, and to what extent they should bind themselves with reference to the future terms of peace.

Colonel House's effort to secure official recognition of the Fourteen Points was therefore bound to meet with stout resistance. To forestall the charge that Mr. Wilson's program was too vague for practical purposes, the Colonel had secured the President's approval for an analytical interpretation of the Fourteen Points prepared specially for the occasion. Nevertheless, there was much protest and argument about specific items, notably about freedom of the seas. Only a thinly veiled threat from House, suggesting that in the event of continued Allied obstruction the President might have to refer the matter to Congress and perhaps conclude a separate peace with Germany, eventually broke the deadlock.[18] The Allies

16 Seymour, "Woodrow Wilson" (*Dictionary of American Biography*, XX, 352–368).

17 Sir C. E. Callwell, *Field Marshal Sir Henry Wilson* (New York, 1929), II, 134, 136, where much stronger words are recorded. See also Willert, *The Road to Safety*, 160, and Rudin, *Armistice 1918*, 167 ff.

18 Seymour, *Intimate Papers* IV, 165 ff.; Stephen Bonsal, *Unfinished Business* (New York, 1944), 2–3; Willert, *The Road to Safety*, 162–163; Joseph C. Grew, *The Turbulent Era* (Boston, 1952) I, 346 ff.

accepted the Fourteen Points as the basis of the forth-coming peace settlement, except for reservations regarding freedom of the seas and reparations. Thereupon the President invited the Germans to send an emissary to conclude an armistice, the terms of which had in the interval been worked out by the Allied military authorities.

It is now generally agreed that the so-called pre-Armistice agreement bound all parties not only morally but legally to make peace on the basis of the Wilsonian program. Thus far, then, the President had been strikingly successful. Although the Allies had with American aid reduced the German military machine to impotence, they had bound themselves not to take advantage of their victory to impose a punitive peace.

But while the President, through Colonel House, was scoring an important point in his relations with European statesmen, he was definitely losing popular support, at least in his own country. In the mid-term election campaign of November, 1918, he made what by common consent was an egregious political error when he called upon those who supported his policy to return Democratic candidates to Congress. His Republican opponents made fullest use of this implication of lack of patriotism on their part and rose to "the loftiest heights of vituperation." The November poll vindicated them by giving them control of both houses of Congress.

Although in fact it would be hard to prove that in November, 1918, even a single Senatorial contest had been fought on the issue of American policy at the peace conference, it was politically at least understandable that the victorious Republicans should have proclaimed the result of the election a repudiation of Wilsonism. Senator Lodge hastened to assure the British Foreign Secretary

(November 25) that it was the overwhelming desire of Americans of all parties that peace terms be imposed on the Germans without discussion. The elections, he asserted, meant popular endorsement of a harsh policy. Former President Roosevelt on his part declared exultantly: "Mr. Wilson and his Fourteen Points and his four supplementary points and his five complementary points and all his utterances every which way have ceased to have any shadow of right to be accepted as expressive of the will of the American people." On December 21 Lodge warned in a public speech that the President's plan of making the constitution of the League of Nations ("that evil thing with the holy name") an integral part of the over-all settlement rested on the theory that the Senate, though possessing the power, never had and would not now dare reject a treaty of peace. The Allies, he continued, should realize that even if the treaty were not rejected, it could be delayed and amended. None but the totally blind could fail to see that the Republicans were taking up the cudgels to beat the life out of Wilsonism. In January, 1919, Lodge told a representative of the *New York Sun* that the League was to be "the biggest Republican issue since the Civil War."[19]

In view of the threatening political storm it may seem strange that the President should have insisted on going abroad to attend the peace conference in person. His decision in this matter has been frequently criticized on the score that his influence over the peacemaking would have been greater had he remained at home. I consider this proposition highly debatable, but in the present

[19] Schriftgiesser, *The Gentleman from Massachusetts,* 298–310; Garraty, *Henry Cabot Lodge,* 343; Willert, *The Road to Safety,* 164. Roosevelt's remarks are quoted in Seymour, *Intimate Papers,* IV, 151.

context I am interested in certain immediate, specific considerations that induced the President to go abroad: firstly, he was profoundly distrustful of his European colleagues; secondly, he believed his presence in Europe essential for the victory of the liberal cause; and thirdly, he expected to be in Europe for only about three weeks during which, in conference with the Allies, the broad lines of the settlement, especially the constitution of a League of Nations, might be laid down, preparatory to discussions with the Germans.

As for the declamations of his Republican opponents, Mr. Wilson obviously underrated their significance. He had no shadow of doubt that he, not Roosevelt nor Lodge, was the exponent of the moral and spiritual forces of the world. Speaking to his staff en route to Europe he observed that for the first time in history peace would be shaped on the opinion of mankind. People were heartily sick of the old system of balance of power and wanted the Powers and the conference to strike out on an entirely new course. In a speech at Manchester (England) on December 30, 1918, he proclaimed: "We are not obeying the mandate of party or politics, we are obeying the mandate of humanity." As for his opponents, he made but little effort to conceal his conviction that most senators were "pygmy-minded." When told of the growing opposition in the upper house, he remarked: "Those Senators do not know what the people are thinking. They are as far from the people, the great mass of our people, as I am from Mars. Indeed, they are out of touch with the thinking, forward-looking masses of people throughout the world."[20]

The President and his staff arrived in Europe just as Mr. Lloyd George and the Conservative party were win-

[20] Bonsal, *Unfinished Business,* 10 ff., 47.

ning a spectacular electoral victory amid shouts of
"Hang the Kaiser" and "Make 'em pay." The political
press in France likewise revealed wide support of a harsh
policy and M. Clemenceau's speech of December 29,
1918, extolling the old system of alliances as the best
guarantee of French security, brought him a huge parliamentary majority. Yet President Wilson was received
with frantic enthusiasm wherever he journeyed in
France, Italy and England. The milling crowds, the
wild acclaim strengthened his conviction that the peoples, in contrast to the politicians, were looking to him
and expecting him to fight for a new and more righteous
world order. The President, almost obsessed by the idea
that European statesmen were banding together to obstruct and defeat his program, was just as deeply persuaded that the masses were with him and that, when the
test came, statesmen would be unable to withstand the
"great compulsion of the Common Conscience."

Actually the reverse proved true. In his *Memoirs* Mr.
Lloyd George confesses that European statemen at first
eyed the President "with a measure of suspicion not un-
mixed with apprehension." They felt that while they
themselves had been dealing with the ghastly realities of
war, he had been "soaring in clouds of serene rhetoric."
They resented his superior attitude, his moralizing and
preaching, in short what they regarded as his megalo-
mania.[21] But they soon discovered his sincerity, his readiness to listen, his consideration for others. British and
French statesmen got along with their American guest
much better than any of them had expected, and agreement on basic matters was reached with remarkably
little difficulty. Mr. Wilson had insisted that the confer-

[21] David Lloyd George, *Memoirs of the Peace Conference* (New
Haven, 1939), I, 139–141; Willert, *The Road to Safety,* 166.

ences of the victorious powers should be of a strictly preliminary character for, as he said, "the general Peace Conference would be a sham if definite conclusions were simply arrived at beforehand and then presented to Germany." Furthermore, he left no doubt that he meant to make the League of Nations the center of the whole program and let everything revolve about that. "Once that is a *fait accompli*," he argued, "nearly all the very serious difficulties will disappear."[22] The British, having concluded that the League was the only thing the President really cared about, agreed that at the conference the League issue should be discussed first.[23] In short, there was no serious difference of opinion, not even on that perennial source of friction, the question of freedom of the seas, which Mr. Wilson did not press.

On the other hand the President was to find, as affairs progressed, that he had nothing like the popular support that he thought he had mobilized. The ovations of December, 1918, which I myself witnessed, were certainly quite unprecedented, quite amazing. They must, I think, be taken as demonstrations of appreciation for what the President and the American people had done to bring the war to a successful conclusion. Or, as Harold Nicolson puts it in his fascinating study of the Peace Conference, the crowds acclaimed the President as the symbol of their victory, not, as Mr. Wilson thought, as the symbol of a new Europe. So far as one can determine, the peoples of the victorious countries had but a vague conception of the Wilsonian program. In general they favored what was good and noble. But when the concrete terms of the settlement were in question, they

[22] Seymour, *Intimate Papers*, IV, 251–252; Willert, *The Road to Safety*, 177.

[23] Lloyd George, *Memoirs*, I, 114 ff., 185.

wanted to see the Germans get their deserts and hoped to attain their own security at the expense of their defeated enemy. In the United States, where there was no demand for territorial or even economic gains, there was strong sentiment for a Draconian peace. "I really believe that there would be something like an uprising if a compromise peace were seriously proposed," reported a foreign correspondent in November, 1918.[24]

This leads me to reflect briefly on a problem which underlies all international relations in this age of democracy. It has by now become patent that modern war, that is total war, requires the mobilization of all the capabilities of the nations engaged. War production must be maximized, and, above all, the population must be stimulated to almost superhuman effort. This can be achieved only by arousing fear, by stirring aggressive impulses, by inciting hatred, by encouraging vindictiveness. Once popular passions have been inflamed, it becomes impossible to extinguish them. In a word, the emotional tension necessary to win a war destroys all chance of concluding a reasonable peace in the hour of victory. Democracies may be basically peace-loving, but once provoked to fight they find it extremely difficult to forgive their adversary and much prefer to fight it out to the bitter end. Looking back on the Peace Conference of 1919 Harold Nicolson comes to this conclusion: "Given the atmosphere of the time, given the passions aroused in all democracies by four years of war, it would have been impossible even for supermen to devise a peace of moderation and righteousness."[25]

[24] Willert, *The Road to Safety*, 164.

[25] Harold Nicolson, *Peacemaking, 1919* (New York, 1933), 7; George F. Kennan, *American Diplomacy, 1900–1950* (Chicago, 1951), 65.

Sensing this, President Wilson had tried desperately to keep his country out of the war. "Once lead this people into war," he remarked prophetically on the eve of American intervention, "and they'll forget there ever was such a thing as tolerance."[26] As aforesaid, war madness did in fact seize the American public in the winter of 1918–1919, at which time the elections in Britain showed that the populations of Europe too were calling for terms that bore but little resemblance to the new order of the idealists' dreams.

The Peace Conference, which opened in Paris in mid-January, 1919, was, you will recall, intended to be an informal preliminary meeting of the victors to determine the broad lines of the settlement as they were then to be discussed with the Germans in a formal Peace Congress. President Wilson, who had expressed himself firmly against a dictated peace, expected the preliminary discussions to last only a few weeks, during which time he hoped at least to float the League of Nations. This to him was the crucial matter. All else could wait. In the words of Colonel House, the rest was "simply a question of boundaries and what not, which had been the subject matter of peace conferences since time immemorial."[27] These problems could be worked out later by experts. Such errors or injustices as afterward became evident could be rectified by the League. This was to be one of the organization's prime purposes, as the President saw it.[28]

[26] Quoted by Thomas A. Bailey, *Woodrow Wilson and the Lost Peace* (New York, 1944), 309.

[27] Seymour, *Intimate Papers,* IV, 300, 321.

[28] For details see David H. Miller, "The Making of the League of Nations," in House and Seymour, *What Really Happened at Paris,* chap. XVII, and F. P. Walters, *A History of the League of*

Allied statesmen raised no serious objection to Mr. Wilson's proposals that the League issue be first on the agenda and that the constitution or Covenant of the League be made an integral part of the Treaty. The President was chosen chairman of the committee to draft the Covenant and promptly threw himself into this congenial assignment. He quickly abandoned his earlier plan for a loose and simple system—hardly more than an exalted ambassadorial conference—and adopted the basic provisions presented by the British who, as Lloyd George was later at pains to point out, had done much more in the way of planning than had Mr. Wilson.[29] After ten strenuous sessions in about as many days, the President was able in mid-February to lay before a plenary session of the Conference a first draft of the Covenant, which had received the unanimous approval of his committee. He thereupon departed almost at once for home, intending to explain the League to the country and to lay the groundwork for ratification of the Treaty by the Senate.

In the course of his brief stay in the United States Mr. Wilson made a programmatic speech at Boston and conferred at some length with Congressional leaders in Washington. He was much disappointed by the attitude of Senator Lodge and other Republicans, who were highly critical of the draft Covenant. Lodge, a loyal Harvardian, took malicious delight in playing the schoolmaster to the former Nassau President: "As an English composition," he remarked, "it does not rank high. It might get by at Princeton, but certainly not at Har-

Nations (New York, 1952), I, chap. IV; Harold Nicolson, Peacemaking, 1919, 53 ff., 92.

[29] Lloyd George, Memoirs, I, 153.

vard."[30] The "crudeness and looseness of expression," he commented, would inevitably lead to controversy. He and his associates indicated that unless the draft were amended so as to ensure against League intervention in domestic issues like the tariff and immigration, and to safeguard the Monroe Doctrine explicitly, there would be determined opposition and obstruction.[31]

The President did not at first take senatorial objections seriously. He opposed amendments on the grounds that they were bound to provoke similar demands for changes from other powers. He was still sure that American public opinion favored the League by an "overwhelming majority," although a poll of newspaper opinion taken in March, 1919, revealed substantial opposition and considerable uncertainty and hesitation. Eventually, however, he thought better of it. On his return to Paris in mid-March he succeeded in piloting the desired amendments through his committee. It was his first significant concession to national pressure, and the records of the Conference suggest that this first yielding on his part not only estranged many of his most devoted followers, but did in fact generate greater and greater pressure from other powers for corresponding concessions in their own national interest. In order to marshal for the League project the support necessary for success, it became more and more imperative to make sacrifices on other issues.[32]

I do not propose to analyze, even briefly, the main features of the European settlement. For various reasons

[30] Bonsal, *Unfinished Business*, 275.
[31] Garraty, *Henry Cabot Lodge*, 350-351. Seymour, *Intimate Papers*, IV, 385.
[32] Seymour, *Intimate Papers*, IV, 410–411; Bonsal, *Unfinished Business*, 144, 153, 166.

the Conference became enmeshed in more and greater complications. This was due in large measure to the disintegration of the European system, to the growing threat of Bolshevism, to economic want and even starvation. In part, however, the trouble stemmed from lack of clarity in procedure and organization. The "Preliminary Conference" went on and on because of delays in the completion of the military clauses of the Treaty. As one territorial decision was added to another, it became clear that the resulting agreements would not be what the President had expected, "a sort of exalted Armistice," but a full-fledged treaty which, on the American side, would require the approval of the Senate. So, imperceptibly, the preliminary discussions between the victors turned into the real peace conference, which arrived at the terms of peace without the Germans being allowed to take part in the negotiations. This was what the French had always wanted and what the President had always objected to. Now he was to become a party to the "dictated" peace almost without knowing how this had come about.[33]

With respect to the treatment of specific issues the American delegation had worked out neither a program nor a procedure. It will be remembered that the President had originally thought of territorial problems as

[33] Seymour, *Intimate Papers,* IV, 354, 356, 373. From these records it appears that the idea of a preliminary peace persisted as late as April 25 and was never formally dropped. See also Nicolson, *Peacemaking, 1919,* 95 ff., who explains that in the general confusion, the victors "forgot about the enemy," and Ludwig Zimmermann, "Die Pariser Friedenskonferenz von 1919 und die Neuordnung Europas" (*Die Welt als Geschichte,* XIII, 1953, 109–136), who argues that by leaving the terms of the Armistice to the military the negotiators made a dictated peace almost inevitable.

matters for the Europeans to settle amongst themselves. The whole American approach was therefore critical and cautionary rather than constructive. American experts were members of the numerous special committees, but they received no regular instructions and their activities were not co-ordinated. Furthermore, many of them, including the President and Colonel House, were themselves affected by the war fever. To a man they seem to have accepted without question the doctrine of German sole responsibility for the war, which then served as justification for many of the most severe provisions of the settlement. Pressed for time and swamped by a multiplicity of issues, Mr. Wilson and his staff made concessions and compromises which, when put together, contributed to a peace that in many respects violated the pre-Armistice agreements and was certainly harsh if not unjust.[34]

As the Treaty neared completion, President Wilson and Colonel House, like Mr. Lloyd George and other British statesmen, realized that the terms were too drastic and that the Treaty fell far short of the proclaimed ideal. The President was heartsick over the compromises he had made, and found consolation only in the thought that the League of Nations, reconsidering objectionable items of the Treaty in circumstances of greater tranquillity, would make the necessary revisions. "I feel that we had best clean up a lot of rubbish with the least friction," counseled Colonel House, "and let the League of Nations and the new era do the rest." The President himself explained that the Treaty, like all

[34] Nicolson, *Peacemaking, 1919,* 43, gives a succinct review of the terms as they compared with the Fourteen Points. See also p. 112 for the shock with which some members discovered that the terms in aggregate were more Draconian than any single item.

human documents, might be imperfect, "but with the Covenant an integral and inseparable part of the Treaty, the mechanism to perfect our work, to adjust it to the needs of the situations which may arise, will be close at hand."[35]

President Wilson has been severely criticized by an eminent American diplomat, George F. Kennan, for having allowed himself to be so blinded by the vision of a new world that he failed to see the need to concern himself with the practical settlement of European problems.[36] This criticism would have less validity if the League had been able to operate under American leadership and with Germany as an original member, as the President intended. It might then have indeed performed the function envisaged for it. Unfortunately, however, and contrary to all expectations, the United States Senate took the Covenant and "flung it into the gutter to rot," to borrow Mr. Lloyd George's malicious phrase.[37]

The story of the dramatic struggle between President Wilson and the majority leaders of the Senate over ratification of the Treaty of Versailles, including the Covenant of the League, is certainly one of the most disheartening chapters of American history. The main features of the episode are well known and I do not propose to examine the details. Suffice it to point out that present-day students of the period are all but unanimous in the conviction that even though the country found the harsh peace treaty unobjectionable, it was generally favorable to the League project and prepared to assume

[35] Seymour, *Intimate Papers,* IV, 454, 474, 488; Bonsal, *Unfinished Business,* 206, 215; Nicolson, *Peacemaking, 1919,* 92.
[36] Kennan, *American Diplomacy,* 68.
[37] Lloyd George, *Memoirs,* I, 153.

the responsibilities of membership in a world organization. Furthermore, the opposing political parties were not so far apart that a satisfactory compromise could not have been reached.

The conflict hinged on the so-called Lodge Reservations, which were firmly supported by all Republican Senators excepting for a dozen irreconcilables—the "Battalion of Death," led by Senators Borah and Hiram Johnson—who would have none of the Covenant on any terms. But these Lodge Reservations, even the crucial one bearing on Article X (provisions for action to enforce peace), were essentially declaratory. They may have been unnecessary, but they were also innocuous. Constitutional lawyers tell us that they would have left the structure of the League intact and would not have interfered at all with its workings.[38] Furthermore, there is good reason to believe that if the Treaty had been ratified with these reservations, the British, French, and other powers signatories of the peace treaty would have accepted them, if only to secure the active participation of the United States in the new world organization. One's sense of tragedy becomes even deeper on learning that President Wilson at one juncture made his own version of the four most important reservations, and that this version differed but slightly from that of Lodge.

How, then, is this woeful struggle to be explained? Partly, no doubt, in terms of rank partisanship. The Republicans were determined to deprive the President and his party of sole credit for the new order. If there was to be a League, it was to have a Republican as well as a Democratic imprint. Even more important was the personal factor—the long-standing mutual hostility between

[38] Miller, "The Making of the League of Nations," in House and Seymour, *What Really Happened at Paris,* 424.

the two scholars in politics, President Wilson and Senator Henry Cabot Lodge. The latter had been an early proponent of the idea of a League with teeth in it, but his ardor had cooled when the President adopted the project. Lodge always maintained that he was not opposed to the idea of a League but only to the Covenant as submitted by Mr. Wilson. The fact is that he was consumed by what his latest biographer calls "a festering dislike" of the President and that he was determined to utilize his position as chairman of the Committee on Foreign Relations and leader of the Republican majority to force the President to accept his reservations. Lodge capitalized Mr. Wilson's known disdain for many members of the upper house and for that august body itself. He considered the President's failure to consult the Senate before naming the peace delegation "unforgivably insulting," and left no stone unturned in his effort to encompass his fall.[39]

In retrospect no one will deny that President Wilson underestimated the power of the Senate and the determination of his opponents. He was misled by the fact that in all its history the Senate had never rejected a peace treaty. Even on his return from Europe in July, 1919, he refused to believe that it would dare reject so important a commitment as the Versailles Treaty. Colonel House urged a conciliatory attitude, but Mr. Wilson went home determined to fight. He would accept certain reservations of an interpretive nature if voted separately from the resolution of ratification, but not as an integral part of the ratification, as Lodge insisted. Such reservations, the President argued on what appear to be doubt-

[39] Both Schriftgiesser, *The Gentleman from Massachusetts,* and Garraty, *Henry Cabot Lodge,* discuss the whole matter with balance and good judgment.

ful grounds, would be tantamount to nullification, and would require resubmission of the Treaty to the signatories. This step, dishonoring to him and humiliating to the country, might reopen the whole peace negotiations. Firmly convinced as ever that the people, if informed of the facts, would support him, he set out on a strenuous speaking tour through the West which ended, late in September, with his total collapse. For many weeks he was almost completely incapacitated—unable to confer even with the Democratic leadership of the Senate.

The Treaty with the Lodge Reservations was voted down for the first time on November 19, 1919, the Republican irreconcilables joining with the Democrats to make a tally of 39 for and 55 against. On the second occasion (March 19, 1920) after endless effort to find a compromise, 21 Democrats bolted and voted with the Republicans for the reservations, making a tally of 49 for and 35 against. A majority, therefore, voted for ratification with reservations, but fell seven votes short of the required two thirds. Since it was well known that most Democratic Senators would have voted for ratification with reservations if the President had not remained adamant against all compromise, it is clear that Mr. Wilson was himself a prime agent of the League's failure.

It has been said that he should not be judged by his conduct in this struggle with the Senate—that he was in a state of nervous and physical collapse so complete that he was in no position to judge the need for compromise.[40] Perhaps so, but the fact remains that his mind was clear and that he had showed no greater disposition to make concessions before his breakdown than he did

[40] Seymour, "Woodrow Wilson," in *Dictionary of American Biography*, XX, 352–368.

afterward. His position remained perfectly consistent throughout, and we can only assume that, leaving aside the personal factor, he could not bring himself to have the charter of the new order made a political football, or permit the United States to lead the way to the gradual subversion of the organization through encumbering reservations and exceptions.

Rather than jeopardize all that had been accomplished, he decided to bide his time, convinced that the rightness of his cause would assure its triumph and the weight of public opinion would eventually make itself felt. Even the presidential election of November, 1920, which ended in a Republican landslide and brought from Lodge the jubilant exclamation: "We have torn up Wilsonism by the roots," failed to shake the President's confidence. At Christmas, 1922, he assured one of his friends that he had not the slightest doubt of the ultimate acceptance of the Covenant: "The world will not commit suicide," he added prophetically and, let us hope, correctly.[41] So also in his last public appearance, on Armistice Day, 1923, he declared: "I am not one of those that have the least anxiety about the triumph of the principles I have stood for. I have seen fools resist Providence before, and I have seen their destruction. . . . That we shall prevail is as sure as that God reigns."[42]

Meanwhile his prediction has come true. The United States is a member of the United Nations and, in the Korean crisis of 1950, assumed obligations onerous beyond any that could have been contemplated thirty years ago. But it is impossible, looking back, not to re-

[41] Bonsal, *Unfinished Business,* 283.
[42] Quoted by Thomas A. Bailey, *Woodrow Wilson and the Great Betrayal* (New York, 1945), 350.

gard as tragedy the absence of the United States from
the League of Nations in the crucial period between the
World Wars, for there is no reason to believe that, with
active American participation, the new world order
might not have performed efficiently many of the func-
tions assigned to it by the Covenant.

All in all, Woodrow Wilson had his weaknesses and
these weaknesses bred mistakes. As I see it his failings
were mostly those of his generation—exaggerated idealism, superiority complex, ignorance of world affairs
resulting from isolation, failure to recognize the true national interest and to assume the obligations demanded
by it. But Woodrow Wilson had also his strengths—his
adherence to principle, his conception of political mo-
rality, his faith in his country's mission to advance freedom and justice, his advocacy of a conciliatory peace,
and his devotion to the idea of a new world order to
provide security and exorcise war. He saw that the days
of American isolation were over and that his country
must play an appropriate part in the affairs of the world.
The European War revealed to him the vision of American leadership. He sensed the dangers involved in victory, and, even after the United States had been forced to
enter the conflict, he threw the weight of his own and
his country's influence on the side of moderation and
magnanimity. No man ever expressed more clearly the
dangers of a dictated, punitive peace, or set forth more
convincingly the need for world organization.

All these are matters of significance now as they were
then, and we may rightly bemoan President Wilson's
failure to attain all his objectives. In one of his earliest
and most revealing addresses, his Commencement Address at the University of Tennessee in 1890, he remarked of Edmund Burke, whom he greatly admired,

that he had been not only wise too soon, but wise too much, for "he went on from the wisdom of today to the wisdom of tomorrow, to the wisdom which is for all time." It was impossible, he added, that Burke should have been followed so far, for "men want the wisdom they are expected to apply to be obvious and conveniently limited in amount."[43] This criticism, so it seems to me, might be made of Woodrow Wilson himself as well as of Edmund Burke. Is it not possible that he set his sights too high; that the grandeur of his principles, the strength of his convictions, and the depth of his faith were such as to blind him at times to the meanness of human nature and the realities of political life? I will not attempt to answer these questions, but they are obviously worth pondering as we review and weigh the career of a great man and an inspiring statesman.

[43] Woodrow Wilson, "Leaders of Men," edited by T. H. Vail Motter (Princeton, 1952).